International Labour and Employment Compliance Handbook

www.kluwerlawonline.com

Labour and Employment Compliance in South Africa

International Bar Association

Labour and Employment Compliance in South Africa

Eighth Edition

Susan Stelzner[†]
Stuart Harrison
Brian Patterson
Zahida Ebrahim

This publication is part of the International Labour and Employment Compliance Handbook, available on www.kluwerlawonline.com

Editors: Salvador del Rey and Robert J. Mignin
Associate Editor: Juan Bonilla

the global voice of the legal profession

Wolters Kluwer

Published by:
Kluwer Law International B.V.
PO Box 316
2400 AH Alphen aan den Rijn
The Netherlands
E-mail: international-sales@wolterskluwer.com
Website: lrus.wolterskluwer.com

Sold and distributed in North, Central and South America by:
Wolters Kluwer Legal & Regulatory U.S.
7201 McKinney Circle
Frederick, MD 21704
United States of America
Email: customer.service@wolterskluwer.com

Sold and distributed in all other countries by:
Air Business Subscriptions
Rockwood House
Haywards Heath
West Sussex
RH16 3DH
United Kingdom
Email: international-customerservice@wolterskluwer.com

ISBN 978-94-035-2504-4

e-Book: ISBN 978-94-035-2505-1
web-PDF: ISBN 978-94-035-2510-5

All listed titles are also available on lrus.wolterskluwer.com

1. Argentina: Julio César Stefanoni Zani & Enrique Alfredo Betemps, *Labour and Employment Compliance in Argentina, 8th edition*, 2020 (ISBN 978-94-035-2491-7)
2. Australia: John Tuck, Stephen Price, Rosemary Roach, Jack de Flamingh, Nicholas Ellery & Nick Le Mare, *Labour and Employment Compliance in Australia, 5th edition*, 2020 (ISBN 978-94-035-2810-6)
3. Belgium: Chris Van Olmen, *Labour and Employment Compliance in Belgium, 5th edition*, 2020 (ISBN 978-94-035-2780-2)
4. Brazil: Rodrigo Seizo Takano, Andrea Giamondo Massei & Murilo Caldeira Germiniani, *Labour and Employment Compliance in Brazil, 7th edition*, 2020 (ISBN 978-94-035-2494-8)
5. Canada: Kevin Coon & Adrian Ishak, *Labour and Employment Compliance in Canada, 2nd edition*, 2014 (ISBN 978-90-411-5637-2)
6. Chile: Gerardo Otero A., Maria Dolores Echeverria F., Macarena López M. & María de los Ángeles Fernández S., *Labour and Employment Compliance in Chile, 8th edition*, 2020 (ISBN 978-94-035-2511-2)
7. China: King & Wood Mallesons, *Labour and Employment Compliance in China, 5th edition*, 2018 (ISBN 978-94-035-0400-1)
8. France: Pascale Lagesse, *Labour and Employment Compliance in France, 8th edition*, 2020 (ISBN 978-94-035-2544-0)
9. Germany: Gerlind Wisskirchen & Martin Lützeler, *Labour and Employment Compliance in Germany, 8th edition*, 2020 (ISBN 978-94-035-2783-3)
10. India: Manishi Pathak, *Labour and Employment Compliance in India, 8th edition*, 2020 (ISBN 978-94-035-2534-1)
11. Ireland: Duncan Inverarity & Ailbhe Dennehy, *Labour and Employment Compliance in Ireland, 7th edition*, 2020 (ISBN 978-94-035-2803-8)
12. Israel: Pnina Broder-Manor, Helen Raziel & Ilan Winder, *Labour and Employment Compliance in Israel, 7th edition*, 2020 (ISBN 978-94-035-2790-1)
13. Italy: Angelo Zambelli, *Labour and Employment Compliance in Italy, 8th edition*, 2020 (ISBN 978-94-035-2514-3)
14. Japan: Yoshikazu Sugino, *Labour and Employment Compliance in Japan, 8th edition*, 2020 (ISBN 978-94-035-2501-3)
15. Republic of Korea: Sang Wook Cho, Soojung Lee & Christopher Mandel, *Labour and Employment Compliance in the Republic of Korea, 6th edition*, 2020 (ISBN 978-94-035-2521-1)
16. Mexico: Oscar De La Vega Gómez, *Labour and Employment Compliance in Mexico, 8th edition*, 2020 (ISBN 978-94-035-2820-5)
17. The Netherlands: Els de Wind & Cara Pronk, *Labour and Employment Compliance in the Netherlands, 4th edition*, 2018 (ISBN 978-94-035-0470-4)
18. Poland: Barbara Jóźwik, *Labour and Employment Compliance in Poland, 8th edition*, 2020 (ISBN 978-94-035-2551-8)
19. Russia: Anna-Stefaniya Chepik, *Labour and Employment Compliance in Russia*, 2013 (ISBN 978-90-411-4925-1)

20. Saudi Arabia: Sara Khoja & Sarit Thomas, *Labour and Employment Compliance in Saudi Arabia, 3rd edition,* 2020 (ISBN 978-94-035-2524-2)
21. South Africa: Susan Stelzner, Stuart Harrison, Brian Patterson & Zahida Ebrahim, *Labour and Employment Compliance in South Africa, 8th edition,* 2020 (ISBN 978-94-035-2504-4)
22. Spain: Salvador del Rey, Ana Campos & Sergi Gálvez Duran, *Labour and Employment Compliance in Spain, 8th edition*, 2020 (978-94-035-2541-9)
23. Turkey: Sertaç Kökenek & Elif Nur Çakır Vurgun, *Labour and Employment Compliance in Turkey, 6th edition*, 2020 (ISBN 978-94-035-2793-2)
24. United Arab Emirates: Sara Khoja & Sarit Thomas, *Labour and Employment Compliance in the United Arab Emirates, 7th edition*, 2020 (ISBN 978-94-035-2531-0)
25. United Kingdom: Ed Mills, Ailie Murray, Anna West, Gareth Walls, Emmie Ellison & Elliot English, *Labour and Employment Compliance in the United Kingdom*, 2020 (ISBN 978-94-035-2800-7)
26. United States: Andrew J. Boling, Amy de La Lama, William Dugan, Chris Guldberg, Brian Hengesbaugh, Robert J. Mignin, John M. Murphy & Ginger Partee, *Labour and Employment Compliance in the United States, 6th edition*, 2020 (ISBN 978-94-035-2813-7)

International Bar Association
The Global Voice of the Legal Profession

The International Bar Association (IBA), established in 1947, is the world's leading organization of international legal practitioners, bar associations and law societies. The IBA influences the development of international law reform and shapes the future of the legal profession throughout the world. It has a membership of over 40,000 individual lawyers and almost 200 bar associations and law societies spanning all continents. It has considerable expertise in providing assistance to the global legal community.

Grouped into two divisions – the Legal Practice Division and the Public and Professional Interest Division – the IBA covers all practice areas and professional interests, providing members with access to leading experts and up-to-date information. Through the various committees of the divisions, the IBA enables an interchange of information and views among its members as to laws, practices and professional responsibilities relating to the practice of business law around the globe. Additionally, the IBA's high-quality publications and world-class conferences provide unrivalled professional development and network-building opportunities for international legal practitioners and professional associates.

The IBA's Bar Issues Commission provides an invaluable forum for IBA member organisations to discuss all matters relating to law at an international level.

The IBA's Human Rights Institute (IBAHRI) works across the Association, to promote, protect and enforce human rights under a just rule of law, and to preserve the independence of the judiciary and the legal profession worldwide.

Other institutions established by the IBA include the Southern Africa Litigation Centre and the International Legal Assistance Consortium.

Employment and Industrial Relations Law Committee

The aims of the committee are to develop and exchange knowledge of employment and industrial relations law and practice. Members support each other through the provision of innovative ideas and practical assistance on day-to-day issues. In addition, through its journal and through presentations, conferences, the committee ensures the dissemination of up-to-date law and practice in this highly important business area.

International Bar Association Global Employment Institute

The IBA Global Employment Institute (IBA GEI) was formed in early 2010 for the purpose of developing for multinationals and worldwide institutions a global and strategic approach to the key legal issues in the human resources and human capital fields.

Drawing on the resources and expertise of the IBA membership, the IBA GEI will provide a unique contribution in the field of employment, discrimination and immigration law, on a diverse range of global issues, to private and public organizations throughout the world. The IBA GEI is designed to enhance the management, performance and productivity of these organizations and help achieve best practice in their human capital and management functions from a strategic perspective.

The IBA GEI will become the leading voice and authority on global HR issues by virtue of having a number of the world's leading labour and employment practitioners in its ranks, and the support and resource of the world's largest association of international lawyers.

Further information

International Bar Association, 4th Floor, 10 St Bride Street, London EC4A 4AD, United Kingdom, Tel: +44 (0)20 7842 0090, Fax: +44 (0)20 7842 0091, E-mail: member@int-bar.org, www.ibanet.org

About the International Labour and Employment Compliance Handbook

From 1976 through 1988, the International Bar Association and Kluwer Law International published the groundbreaking International Handbook on Contracts of Employment. This Handbook provided one of the first global overviews of the law of the international employment relationship.

Since publishing the first edition, globalization of business has created an increased demand for knowledge of labor and employment laws throughout the world. Therefore, along with Kluwer, we decided to publish an updated Handbook which we have titled the International Labour and Employment Compliance Handbook.

This new Handbook was intended to be a practical guide by providing a general overview of key labor and employment issues in multiple jurisdictions. Each chapter was written so that it is easy to understand by lawyers and non-lawyers alike. Each country author has also followed a standard outline to assist readers in analysing employment issues in each country.

The first edition of this new Handbook included nineteen (19) different countries.

This Handbook would not have been possible without the help and assistance of many people. Most importantly, the individual country authors are all distinguished legal practitioners who spent considerable time drafting and revising their country reports to meet difficult deadlines. We thank each of them. Our friends at Kluwer, especially Ewa Szkatula, have done a wonderful job in keeping the editors and the authors on schedule. Finally, we want to also express our gratitude to Cuatrecasas, Gonçalves Pereira, and Baker & McKenzie LLP for their valuable assistance in the coordination and organization of this project. Our warmest thanks to each of them.

Because of the success of the Handbook,Wolters Kluwer Law & Business decided to publish each country report also as a separate book to give a choice in obtaining the information. We hope this new format will be a helpful and useful resource just like the Handbook. Both formats are available in print and online.

The Editors

Salvador del Rey Guanter
Robert J. Mignin

March 2013

Table of Contents

South Africa

AUTHORS

Susan Stelzner

Susan Stelzner was a long-standing practising attorney and director in the Employment Law department of ENSafrica. She tragically passed away on 5 January 2011, but this chapter continues to reflect her prior invaluable contribution, and it is dedicated to her memory.

Stuart Harrison

Stuart Harrison is an Executive at ENSafrica in the Employment Law department. He specializes in all aspects of employment law, including executive appointments and dismissals, disciplining employees involved in procurement irregularities and who contravene the Public Finance Management Act, as well as restraint of trade matters.

He has acted and appeared for clients in various litigious matters in the labour courts, High Court and the CCMA (Commission for Conciliation, Mediation and Arbitration), and he has conducted extensive eviction litigation in the Land Claims Court.

Stuart's experience includes drafting split employment contracts for employees rendering services in multiple jurisdictions, litigation against former executives for the recovery of unauthorized expenditure incurred in breach of fiduciary duties, test case litigation on second generation outsourcing, drafting agreements for clients with labour brokers and preparing and revising constitutions for employers' organizations and bargaining councils. He has also experience in drafting bargaining council main agreements, dealing with the eviction of dismissed employees and other occupiers under the onerous security of tenure legislation and litigating on discrimination law. He has also worked extensively on issues around restructuring in the public sector and the employment law consequences relating to mergers and acquisitions. He has an extensive advisory experience, having assisted in dealing with disciplinary, poor performance, absenteeism and other forms of incapacity matters and rooting out theft rings operating within workforces, as well as successfully running large-scale retrenchment exercises for employers. He has also experience in employee benefits and pension law.

He is the author of the chapter on pension law in Juta's annual labour law publication. He is the co-author of chapters on South African labour law for a number of international comparative employment law publications, such as the *Littler Mendelson Guide to International Employment and Labour Law, the Law Business Research's Employment Law Review* and *the Centre for International Legal Studies' International Employment Law* publication. He has also contributed to *Labour Law for Managers: A Practical Handbook*. He has served as an independent trustee for commercial umbrella funds as well as pension, provident, preservation and retirement annuity funds. Stuart regularly presents at client seminars, training courses, workshops, and he has been a speaker at various public seminars and conferences on numerous issues, including labour brokers, second generation outsourcing, white-collar crime, pension law and ensuring legal and tax compliance in employment contracts and policies.

Stuart is recognized as a leading/recommended lawyer by: Chambers Global Guide 2020, 2019, 2018, 2017, 2016, 2015 – Employment (South Africa); The Legal 500 EMEA 2019, 2018, 2017, 2016, 2015 – Labour and Employment (South Africa); Best Lawyers® 2020, 2019, 2018, 2017, 2016 – Labour and Employment (South Africa); Who's Who Legal 2019, 2016 – Labour and Employment (South Africa).

ADDRESS

1 North Wharf Square
Loop Street
Cape Town
South Africa
Tel.: + 2721 410 2552
E-mail: sharrison@ENSafrica.com
Web: www.ENSafrica.com

Brian Patterson

Brian Patterson is Head of ENSafrica's Employment department. He specializes in integrated employment solutions, international split employment contracts, global mobility, executive terminations, restructuring and retrenchments, transfers of business, employment equity and unfair discrimination, collective bargaining, employment-related pension law matters, and drafting and enforcement of restraint of trade agreements, as well as the law relating to confidentiality and privacy.

Brian has done extensive African employment law work and significant international employment law work in the United States and the United Kingdom (UK) and for many overseas law firms. He is qualified in South Africa and the UK.

Brian has acted for numerous African and international clients and has provided advice to corporate clients in most sectors, including the financial services, retail, hospitality/gaming, pharmaceutical, mining, metal engineering, ITC and chemical industries. He has also dealt with the South African aspects of restructuring/mergers of multinationals in respect of a number of jurisdictions.

In addition, Brian's experience includes giving tactical and strategic individual and collective employment law advice, and he has extensive litigious and corporate employment law experience. He also engages in alternative dispute resolution mechanisms when necessary.

Brian has been involved with some of the leading employment law cases reported in Southern Africa since the inception of employment law, and he has personally argued many matters in the Labour Court and the Labour Appeal Court (LAC). Brian has also acted as a judge of the Labour Court and was an assessor of the LAC.

Brian is the co-author of the South African chapter of *the International Labour and Employment Compliance Handbook* and *The Employment Law Review* and has contributed articles in many local and international publications.

He is a regular speaker on employment and labour law issues and has appeared on many television programmes over the years.

Brian is recognized as a leading/recommended lawyer by Chambers Global Guiden 2020, 2019, 2018, 2017, 2016, 2015 – Employment (South Africa); The Legal 500 EMEA 2019, 2018, 2017, 2016, 2015 – Labour and Employment (South Africa); Who's Who Legal 2019, 2016 – Labour and Employment (South Africa); Best Lawyers® 2020, 2019, 2018, 2017, 2016 – Labour and Employment (South Africa) and Employee and Benefits Lawyers of the year for 2020.

ADDRESS

The MARC | Tower 1
129 Rivonia Road
Sandton
Johannesburg

South Africa
Tel.: + 2711 269 7953
E-mail: bpatterson@ENSafrica.com
Web: www.ENSafrica.com

Zahida Ebrahim

Zahida Ebrahim is an Executive in ENSafrica's Dispute Resolution department, and heads up the firm's immigration unit.

She offers an extensive range of immigration and civic services to individuals and multinational companies, including large corporates and top-tier South African and international companies, as well as to various business chambers and professional bodies.

Zahida's specialist immigration knowledge and experience enables her to offer an all-encompassing range of immigration and civic services, including relating to temporary and permanent residence applications; applications for waiver of regulatory requirements; applications to the South African Department of Trade and Industry and the Department of Labour for immigration-related certifications; applications to the South African Qualifications Authority for evaluation of foreign tertiary qualifications; citizenship-related matters, including applications for naturalization, determination of citizenship status and resumption of citizenship; liaison with the Department of Home Affairs and foreign missions, as well as compliance audits and due diligence investigations.

Zahida actively lobbies for immigration reform by preparing representations to the South African Department of Home Affairs on new and proposed legislative changes, including the amendments to South African immigration legislation in May 2014, where she advised various business chambers and professional bodies on their submissions to government. She previously served on a panel of specialist advisors to the Minister of Home Affairs.

In recognition of Zahida's expertise, she has been invited to speak at various immigration law seminars. This includes:

- AILA (American Immigration Lawyers Association) (Orlando, Florida, 2019)
- The International Bar Association's Nationality and Immigration Conference (London, 2017).

Zahida has also contributed to a number of texts and publications, including a chapter on immigration issues for *Labour Law for Managers: A Practical Handbook*; the South African chapter in the *Employment Law Review and the Getting the Deal Through Labour and Employment Law* publication, *Global Mobility Handbook*, and Oxford University Press' *Corporate Immigration Guide*.

From a dispute resolution perspective, her experience includes advising on policy wording reviews, compliance with South African insurance legislation, insurance due diligence assessments, as well as high court litigation relating to commercial and insurance disputes.

Zahida is recognized as a leading/recommended lawyer by:

- Business Women's Association's Regional Business Achiever Award 2016 – Professional category.
- Best Lawyers® 2020, 2019 – Immigration (South Africa).
- Who's Who Legal 2019, 2017, 2016 – Immigration (South Africa).

ADDRESS

1 North Wharf Square
Loop Street
Cape Town
South Africa
Tel.: +2721 410 6610
E-mail: zebrahim@ENSafrica.com
Web: www.ENSafrica.com

Legal Compliance in South Africa

1. LEGAL FRAMEWORK: EMPLOYMENT LAWS IN SOUTH AFRICA

The Constitution of the Republic of South Africa guarantees fundamental rights that are relevant to employment and labour, such as privacy and equality. However, section 23 deals specifically with labour relations and confers on 'everyone' the right to fair labour practices. It also provides for freedom of association for workers and employers and the right to participate freely in the activities of a trade union or employer's organization. Under the Constitution, trade unions and employer's organizations have the right to form and join federations and to engage in collective bargaining all of which is regulated under the Labour Relations Act (LRA/Act).

The LRA provides for resolution of labour disputes through the establishment of the Commission for Conciliation Mediation and Arbitration (CCMA), the Labour Court and the Labour Appeal Court (LAC). It provides protection for employees against unfair dismissal and unfair labour practices, and it provides further guidance on these issues in Codes of Good Practice, which are issued under the LRA. The LRA also regulates the employment of atypical employees (e.g., leased workers, part-time and fixed-term employees), dismissals by reason of the operational requirements of the employer (commonly referred to as retrenchments), and the rights of employees in the context of the transfer of a business (or part of a business) as a going concern.

Minimum conditions of employment are regulated by the Basic Conditions of Employment Act (BCEA). The BCEA applies to all employers and employees except State Security Agency members and unpaid volunteers working for charity. The BCEA does not set minimum wages. It regulates the working time, leave, particulars of employment (the minimum details that must be communicated to employees, usually via an employment contract) and the keeping of records regarding remuneration, termination of employment (notice and severance pay). It also prohibits child and forced labour.

A particular sector or industry can regulate its own terms and conditions through a Bargaining Council Agreement, entered into by representative employers and unions in the industry concerned. The Bargaining Council Agreement takes precedence over the BCEA, but there are some limitations in terms of what can be varied by agreement. In addition, the Minister of Labour has the power to make Sectoral Determinations for a sector and area, and a number of such determinations have been made. These set minimum standards and terms for the specified sector and take precedence over the BCEA.

Discrimination and affirmative action issues are regulated by the Employment Equity Act (EEA).

The Occupational Health and Safety Act (OHSA) imposes on all employers a general duty to provide and maintain a working environment that is safe, and without risk to employees' health. In addition, there are a number of specific safety regulations published under the OHSA. Payment for work-related injuries and illnesses is covered by the Compensation for Occupational Injuries and Diseases Act (COIDA).

Unemployment is regulated by the Unemployment Insurance Act (UIA) and the Unemployment Insurance Contributions Act. Retirement funding and medical insurance in South Africa are private unless regulated under a Bargaining Council Agreement or for public sector employers. These benefits are subject to regulation by the Pension Funds Act and the Medical Schemes Act, respectively.

The employment of expatriate employees, save for those who are asylum seekers, refugees or permanent residents, is governed by the Immigration Act No. 13 of 2002 and the Regulations published pursuant thereto. The Department of Home Affairs issues non-binding practice directives which influence the execution and application of the law. The Refugees Act No. 130 of 1998 governs the admission of asylum seekers and refugees, affording refugees and asylum seekers the right to work, study, operate businesses and reside in South Africa.

The South African policy on international migration is set out in the 1999 White Paper on International Migration, and a further White Paper on International Migration was published on 21 July 2017.

A new White Paper on International Migration focusing on the review of legislation, policies and procedures in relation to immigration, was published in the Government Gazette on 14 January 2019.

2. CONTRACTS OF EMPLOYMENT

2.1. Overview

Most employees in South Africa are employed under contracts of employment, which may be written, oral or a combination of both. The parties are generally free to enter into indefinite or fixed-term contracts, although there are restrictions on the use of fixed-term contracts for employees who earn less than a prescribed annual earnings threshold (BCEA earnings threshold).[1] The existence of a common law contract of employment is not a prerequisite, however, for an employee to enjoy statutory employment rights, as the definition of who qualifies as an employee under most South African employment legislation includes persons (excluding independent contractors) who assist in carrying on or conducting the business of the employer, even though they may not be formally employed or remunerated by the employer.

By law, the basic conditions of employment provided for under the BCEA constitute terms of any employment relationship. The contract of employment can provide more favourable terms. Collective agreements can vary contracts of employment, if the employers and employees are bound by the collective agreement, within the limits set by the BCEA, that is, there are some terms that cannot be set at less than those provided by the BCEA even by collective agreement.

2.2. Written Employment Contracts

In practice, most employers in South Africa enter into written employment contracts with their employees. There is no general legal requirement for an employer to have a written contract (subject to a few limited exceptions such as merchant seamen for whom written employment contracts are required under the Merchant Shipping Act, learners who are required to have a written contract pursuant to the Skills Development Act and fixed-term contracts for employees earning less than the BCEA earnings threshold).

The BCEA requires an employer to give its employees notice of key employment terms when the employees commence employment. The employer has to specify the following, in writing:

- the date on which the employment began and the employee's place of work;

1. The Minister of Labour determines this threshold more or less annually in terms of s. 6 of the BCEA. The threshold as at April 2019 is ZAR 205,433.30 per annum.

- the occupation of the employee or a brief description of the work for which the employee is employed;
- the employee's ordinary hours of work and days of work;
- the employee's wage or the rate and method of calculating wages;
- the rate of pay for overtime work;
- how frequently remuneration is paid and any deductions to be made from the employee's remuneration;
- the leave to which the employee is entitled;
- the period of notice required to terminate employment, or if employment is for a specified period, the date when employment is to terminate;
- the period of employment with a previous employer that counts towards the employee's period of employment;
- a list of any other documents that form part of the contract of employment and information on where to obtain copies of the documents.

Written contracts are useful to ensure compliance with the above obligation to provide written particulars of employment and to secure important contractual agreements and consents. Examples of the latter include employee consents (where required) to work overtime and on Sundays and public holidays, employee consents to the employer monitoring e-mails and telecommunications usage by the employee, data privacy-related consents and agreed retirement age.

When any of the above matters change, the written particulars must be revised to reflect the change and supplied to the employee.

In general, foreign workers will require a written contract of employment in support of their work visa application. Recently, the Department of Home Affairs has insisted that the duration of the contract may not exceed the maximum period for which the work visa may be granted under the specific work visa category. This requirement has been contested by many applicants and it is uncertain whether the practice will be upheld if judicially contested. An application for a general work visa must be supported by a written local employment contract signed by both the employer and the employee which stipulates the conditions of employment and confirming these are in line with the labour standards. The contract must be made conditional upon the general work visa being approved. Although a critical skills work visa may be issued for a period of twelve months in the absence of a written contract of employment, a written contract must be submitted to the Department of Home Affairs within twelve months of issuance of the visa. The critical skills work visa is granted for up to five years in alignment with the duration of the employment contract if one is submitted.

2.3. Oral Contracts

As indicated above, legally binding contracts of employment can be concluded orally under South African employment law. Such contracts may be concluded from express, oral communications or tacitly from the conduct of the parties. Thus, in principle, contractual rights for employees can arise from long-standing employment practices at the workplace.

In the limited instances where legislation requires the contract to be in writing, where parties agree on an oral contract but fail to conclude a written agreement, this will not necessarily mean that the oral contract is unenforceable.

2.4. Employee Handbooks

Employee handbooks are not compulsory in South Africa but are commonplace for medium and large employers. Handbooks will generally consist of a range of the employer's more important workplace policies and would typically include policies on hours of work, leave, medical aid and pension arrangements, codes of conduct, anti-harassment/discrimination, grievance and disciplinary procedures.

Some policies are included in handbooks as a result of specific legislative imperatives or recommendations, for example:

- a policy on harassment (including sexual harassment) is often included. The Code of Good Practice on the Handling of Sexual Harassment Cases (a code issued under the EEA) recommends that employers have a sexual harassment policy to fulfil the employer's duties to deal appropriately with sexual harassment cases in the workplace, and an absence of such a policy can increase the risk of the employer being held liable for harassment committed by one of its employees;
- a policy on the use of the employer's communications systems in the workplace (including telephones, e-mails and the internet), which warns employees that their use of such systems may be monitored by the employer and that they, therefore, cannot necessarily expect privacy in relation to their communications on the systems. This policy facilitates compliance with the Regulation of Interception of Communications and Provision of Communication-Related Information Act (ROICA), which regulates the monitoring of such communications.

The handbook can be incorporated into the contract of employment by reference, with the result that the terms of the handbook become contractual rights and obligations which cannot be varied other than by agreement. Alternatively, the handbook policies can be stipulated as not having contractual status but still requiring employees to comply therewith. In the latter instance, a typical statement that would be included in the handbook and in the employment contract would be the following:

> While the terms of the Company Handbook issued from time to time are not contractual terms and conditions of employment and may be amended by the Company in its discretion from time to time, the Employee remains subject to its provisions and is obliged to familiarize him/herself and comply therewith. To the extent that there is any inconsistency between the Contract of Employment and the terms of the Company Handbook, the Contract of Employment will prevail. The Company Handbook is available on the Company's Intranet.

The disadvantage of making the handbook a part of the contract is that employers then need agreement from the employees in order to adapt or modify it. If it is not, then no consent is needed. There are very few instances, if any, where it is an advantage to have a policy a term of the contract. If a firm contractual undertaking is required in a particular instance, this can be achieved by dealing with that specific aspect of the contract.

2.5. Job Descriptions

In industries that are regulated by bargaining councils, the collective agreements concluded by such councils usually contain detailed categorizations of jobs in the industry for which minimum wage rates and other terms and conditions of employment will apply.

Otherwise, brief job descriptions (or at least job titles) are usually provided for in the employee's written contract of employment or in some other written form, but often with a qualification that the functions described will vary from time to time at the employer's discretion, or where circumstances require.

Although a job description is not a formal requirement of the work visa application process, reliance is placed on the job description provided in the written contract of employment in determining that the skills set and function fall within the contemplated parameters for applications for critical skills work visas and to ensure that the job description correlates with the advertisement placed in support of a general work visa application. Similarly, the holder of a critical skills work visa must have a job description which aligns with the skills and qualifications contemplated under the relevant critical skills category.

2.6. Offer Letters

There is no requirement in South Africa for an employer to provide a prospective employee with a written offer letter, but it is common practice. In some cases, the offer letter is expressly conditional upon the conclusion of a formal contract of employment, but in other instances offer letters are not succeeded by a formal contract of employment, and operate as the primary documentary evidence of the employment terms. No offer of employment may be extended to a foreign worker until the necessary labour-market testing has been concluded if such testing is required in support of the work visa process.

2.7. Checklist of Do's and Don'ts

- Conclude written contracts of employment or letters of appointment with employees (in a language that they will understand).
- Check that the employment contract is consistent with any applicable minimum benefits legislation or wage regulation measures (such as the BCEA or applicable collective agreements).
- Include useful employee consents in the contract/letter of appointment.
- Consider whether the employee handbook or company policies should be contractual rights and obligations between the parties, or rather just a non-contractual record of policies, and provide clearly for this in the employment contract and handbook.

3. RECRUITING, INTERVIEWING, SCREENING AND HIRING EMPLOYEES

3.1. Overview

In South Africa, the main law which applies to the recruiting and hiring of employees is the EEA. The EEA seeks to eliminate unfair discrimination in employment and to ensure employment equity in the workplace.

Pursuant to the EEA, it is unlawful to unfairly discriminate, directly or indirectly, against an employee (including a job candidate) in any employment policy or practice on the basis of race, gender, sex, pregnancy, marital status, family responsibility, ethnic or social origin, colour, sexual orientation, age, disability, religion, HIV status, conscience, belief, political opinion, culture, language, birth, or any other arbitrary ground.

Employers have a positive duty to take steps to promote equal opportunity in the workplace by eliminating unfair discrimination in any employment policy or practice.

3.2. Recruiting

In general, employers use various methods to recruit employees, including advertising internally, in newspapers, on the internet or by making use of recruitment agencies. In order to avoid unfair discrimination at the commencement of the recruitment process, it is important to ensure that no group of people is excluded by implication. For example, it would be discriminatory to advertise in a newspaper that only targets a specific race group or gender. However, it would be permissible to target a specific protected class provided doing so could be justified based on the inherent requirements of the job.

An application for a general work visa must be accompanied by a certificate from the Department of Labour confirming that despite a diligent search, the prospective employer has been unable to find a suitable citizen or permanent resident with the requisite qualifications or skills and experience to fill the role.

The Department of Labour requires details and evidence how the position was advertised, including placement of the advert in the national print media, written evidence of labour search from at least one relevant private recruitment agency; written evidence of labour search from traditional leaders/community leaders/ward councillors/community based organization and Non-governmental Organisations, where appropriate; written evidence of labour search from sectoral organizations/professional bodies; proof that the opportunity/vacancy was registered in the Department of Labour's Employment Services for South Africa (ESSA) Database and proof of the outcome of any recruitment from the system, as well as interview notes by the employer indicating the rationale for recruited local citizens not being suitable for the vacant post or reasons for locals not being considered at all.

3.3. Employment Applications

Not all employers in South Africa use application forms. Employers will usually request job applicants to provide a copy of their curriculum vitae and relevant supporting documents. If an employer does use an application form, then it should not collect irrelevant information, especially if it is private or relates to a protected class. Legislation protecting personal information, in the form of the Protection of Personal Information Act (POPI Act), was published in November 2013 but is not yet fully in operation. Once it becomes fully operative, it will place restrictions on what information may be collected from employees and applicants. However, the application form provides a useful place to obtain consent for the collecting of relevant information.

Information gleaned from the curriculum vitae will be used to assess the applicant's suitability for the position and thereafter to compile a short list of possible candidates to be interviewed for the position. The interview may be preceded by a request for more detailed information about the candidate.

3.4. Pre-employment Inquiries

The EEA provides that the recruitment and selection process should be conducted fairly and without unfair discrimination.

Any pre-employment inquiry should have as its aim the assessment of the suitability of the applicant for the available position. Questions should, therefore, focus on the essential elements of the job and the necessary competency specifications. Questions relating to an applicant's race, gender, sex or marital status, for example, should be avoided, save that questions relating to race, gender or disability may be permissible if the position to be filled forms part of the employer's statutory affirmative action plan to affirm employees from statutorily recognized designated groups, such as black people (a statutorily defined term that includes South African citizens who are Africans, Coloureds (a recognized term referring to mixed-race people), Indians and Chinese), women and people with disabilities.

3.5. Pre-employment Tests and Examinations

Skills testing is generally acceptable in South Africa if intended to select applicants who will best satisfy the requirements of the job and to establish whether the applicant does in fact have the skills or qualifications they claim to have.

Skills that are not relevant to the job should not be tested. There should also not be an over-emphasis on an applicant's formal qualifications to the exclusion of other considerations which may qualify the applicant for the job. In this regard, the EEA provides that an employer must assess an applicant's ability to do the job in terms of any one of or any combination of the following factors: formal qualifications; prior learning; relevant experience; or the capacity to acquire, within a reasonable time, the ability to do the job. Failure to consider these factors may give rise to a claim of unfair discrimination.

The EEA prohibits medical testing unless the testing is permitted by legislation or is justifiable in the light of medical facts, employment conditions, social policy, the fair distribution of employee benefits or the inherent requirements of the job. Medical testing is defined very broadly (it includes any question designed to ascertain if the employee has any medical condition) and therefore arguably includes testing for the use of alcohol or drugs, although this issue has not been considered by the courts as yet. Testing is likely to be allowed where a job requires a high degree of vigilance or alertness (e.g., in the case of an employee who is employed as a driver or an employee who operates dangerous machinery).

Medical testing does not appear to include a test for a disability. The Disability Code expressly states that tests to establish the health of a job applicant should be distinguished from tests that assess the ability to perform the essential functions and duties of the advertised position. The employer should first test to see if the applicant can perform the essential functions and duties and thereafter (and once the job offer has been made) test to determine the health status. Functional testing may also be required to determine whether any reasonable accommodation is required.

Justification on the basis of a fair distribution of employee benefits is controversial and untested. The argument for testing would be to protect benefit schemes from being overburdened by employees who have serious or life-threatening diseases. However, an employer who offers benefits such as medical aid as part of the remuneration package must ensure that the scheme does not act unfairly or discriminate in an unfair manner.

Any medical testing that is conducted by the employer is ultimately subject to the rights and freedoms guaranteed to job applicants and employees by the Constitution, although will be tested in the first instance by the legislation designed to give weight to these protections, namely the EEA. Employees have the right to equality, human dignity, freedom and security of the person and privacy. These are important constitutional values in any employment-related medical testing which have to be balanced against the legitimate commercial interests of the employer. As these issues have not yet been tested in court, however, it is difficult to give more specificity.

Queries regarding an applicant's use of prescription drugs may reveal an applicant's confidential medical condition, for example, HIV/AIDS status. Thus, such queries can infringe the applicant's constitutional right to privacy. Such inquiries can also violate the provisions of the EEA. Testing for HIV/AIDS status is specifically regulated and is dealt with in section 20 below.

The confidentiality of any medical information must be protected. That duty rests on any person designated by the employer to administer or safeguard any confidential information acquired during the medical test.

Psychometric testing and other similar assessments of an employee are prohibited unless the employer can show that the test or assessment being used:

- has been scientifically shown to be valid and reliable;
- can be applied fairly to employees;
- is not biased against any employee or group; and
- has been certified by the Health Professions Council of South Africa or any other body which may be authorized by law to certify such tests or assessment.

The Immigration Act and regulations provide that medical reports and chest x-rays must be submitted in support of temporary and permanent residence visa applications. These reports are limited to findings on the applicant's mental health and infectious diseases, including tuberculosis.

3.6. Background, Reference and Credit Checks

While there is no general prohibition against an employer doing background checks on an applicant, employers should not exclude an applicant from employment based on information obtained through background checks which are of no relevance to the advertised position or the suitability of the employee to occupy the position. A code of good practice issued under the EEA provides that an employer should only conduct integrity checks, such as investigating whether the applicant has a criminal record if this is relevant to the requirements of the job. Relying on information obtained through background checks to exclude an applicant from a position may give rise to a claim for indirect unfair discrimination, where it has an unequal and disproportionate impact on individuals from a particular group of people, in particular the specifically protected classes.

The Immigration Act and regulations thereto provide that police clearance certificates must be submitted from all countries where an applicant for temporary or permanent residence has resided for more than a year since their 18th birthday.

There is similarly no prohibition on conducting reference checks, although employers requested to provide information about a job applicant to a potential new employer should enquire whether or not the employee has consented to the release of any information. If they have not consented, the former employer should consider whether the information which it is disclosing is private or in the public domain and whether in releasing information it is using such information for purposes other than that for which it was obtained. This will become more important when POPI becomes operative.

In South Africa, detailed information about a person's credit and financial history (including court judgments) is obtainable from a credit bureau. However, the National Credit Act (NCA) stipulates that a credit bureau can only issue a consumer credit report in certain prescribed circumstances, one being when an employer is considering a candidate for employment in a position that requires trust and honesty and entails the handling of cash or finances, and only with the prior consent of the job applicant.

3.7. Interviewing

An employer must ensure that those persons in the company who are involved in the interview process are trained to avoid even the slightest appearance of unfair discrimination by avoiding inquiries that relate to factors such as an applicant's age, sex, disability, race or religion. As a general rule, before starting the interviewing process, employers should prepare a written job description which defines the position and establishes objective qualifications and criteria to be used to screen and interview applicants to avoid unintended or perceived discrimination. Employers should not ask information which is irrelevant to the job.

It is considered a good practice to prepare a set of questions and to ask the same general questions of all applicants for the same position so that each candidate is assessed on a similar basis. This process would also help an employer to defend its decision if challenged in due course.

Employers should keep notes of the interview process so that it has facts on which to justify its decision if required later.

The general work visa application process requires the submission of interview notes to the Department of Labour in order to secure the required certificate in support of the work visa application.

3.8. Hiring Procedures

A successful applicant should be given a written offer of employment. This is normally done through a letter of appointment or an employment contract. Either way, all the important information relating to the position and the remuneration should be fully set out. Attention should also be drawn to any additional policies and procedures which will govern the employment relationship. The employer should consider whether the offer is conditional or not (e.g., on the obtaining of a work permit or a license of some sort) and if so make this clear in the offer. It is mandatory that offers to foreign nationals be conditional upon their procuring an appropriate work visa.

There is generally no requirement for an employer to notify unsuccessful applicants of the fact that their application has not been successful. It can be a daunting administrative exercise in South Africa where high unemployment attracts a large number of applicants.

Employers should make sure that new hires are registered for unemployment insurance and workman's compensation. There may be administrative processes required to register employees for benefits schemes such as medical aid, life and/or disability insurance and retirement funding.

3.9. Fines and Penalties

If an applicant was unfairly discriminated against by the employer in the hiring process, the applicant could be awarded appropriate damages (the amount deemed by a court as required to compensate the employee for the losses suffered as a result of the unfair discrimination). Other than a complaint of unfair discrimination, an applicant has no general right to challenge the employer's recruiting or hiring process.

Existing employees may challenge the employer's decision not to appoint them to the vacant position by filing an unfair labour practice claim in respect of 'promotion'. Usually, the claim will be based on alleged unfair discrimination, but the employee could also claim that he had some sort of prior claim to tenure in the position (e.g., because he has acted in the position for a period of time or was given an expectation of permanent appointment/promotion). The dispute will then have to be resolved through arbitration. The arbitrator is entitled to make an appropriate award in the circumstances. While this could include appointing the employee to the vacant position, this generally does not happen, as arbitrators are hesitant to second-guess the employer's decision. A more appropriate order may be that the hiring process be redone, but the award could include compensation.

3.10. Checklist of Do's and Don'ts

- Do not unfairly discriminate against job applicants in the hiring process on any of the prohibited grounds of which the more common ones are race, gender, religion or marital status.
- When advertising for positions, care should be taken not to do so in a manner which may result in certain categories of people not having access to the advertisement (e.g., by advertising in a newspaper which has a circulation limited to a particular sector of the community).
- If it is likely that local workers with the necessary skills or qualifications will not be available to fill the position, then it is advisable to comply with

the Department of Labour's specifications in relation to the recruitment of foreign nationals to ensure that their advertisement and labour-market testing parameters are met.
- Before an interview, employers should develop a standard list of questions to elicit job-related information. Try to cover all the key aspects of the job through the range of questions and try to ask the same set of questions of all applicants. This does not preclude discussion that may arise with a particular applicant, for example, in the context of an answer given.
- Employers should train all persons involved in the hiring process about discrimination laws and what can or cannot be asked of an applicant.
- Any pre-employment inquiry should have as its aim the assessment of the suitability of the employee for the available position.
- Medical, psychometric and similar tests should only be undertaken in accordance with the EEA.
- Do not ask questions about alcohol and drug use of applicants for employment unless this information is required due to the inherent requirements of the job.
- Employers should conduct background checks on all applicants prior to an offer of employment being made provided that only relevant information is sought. Be sure to research and verify job references, work history and educational background, as it is not uncommon in South Africa for applicants to attach falsified documents to their applications. Also, check out any apparent gap in an applicant's employment history as this may suggest a period of employment that ended for an unhappy reason (hence, the employee excluded it from his employment history).
- Employers should not exclude an applicant from employment based on information obtained through background checks if the information is of no relevance to the advertised position or the suitability of the employee to occupy the position.

4. MANAGING PERFORMANCE/CONDUCT

4.1. Overview

The employer has the prerogative to set standards of performance and conduct for its employees and to enforce those standards. However, the employer must (in terms of its general obligation under the Constitution and as set out more fully in the LRA and the Code of Good Practice: Dismissal (promulgated under the LRA)) act fairly towards employees while doing so.

The Code of Good Practice: Dismissal contains only a guideline for employers, but its recommendations carry a lot of weight as they form the basis of what the arbitrators and courts consider when assessing the fairness of a dismissal. The Code represents, to a large extent, a codification of what had previously been pronounced by the courts before the promulgation of the LRA in 1995.

Where employers adopt their own policies for managing performance or conduct in the workplace that are more onerous for the employer than the Code's guidelines, the employer will generally be held to the more onerous obligations, so employers should consider the terms of such policies carefully.

The Code sets out different processes for managing misconduct and performance issues. It also suggests that the rules of conduct and standards of performance should be clearly communicated to employees. This is often done through, in the case of conduct rules, a code of conduct (or disciplinary code) and, in the case of performance standards, job descriptions, performance requirements communicated to employees at the time of appointment, as well as Key Performance Areas or targets which may be communicated on a regular basis as the employment relationship progresses.

The Code contemplates a system of progressive discipline for misconduct that is aimed primarily at correcting unacceptable behaviour. Dismissal is reserved for cases of serious misconduct or repeated transgressions of the same or a similar nature where warnings have not corrected the behaviour. Warnings should be recorded in the employee's personnel file. Where a written warning is issued, the employee should be given a copy and asked to acknowledge receipt. This system is generally followed by employers as it is the system endorsed by the courts and by arbitrators.

4.2. Coaching and Counselling

For poor performance, the Code contemplates a process of evaluation, instruction, guidance, counselling or training (where reasonable and appropriate), and a reasonable opportunity to improve before it becomes acceptable to terminate for poor performance. What is reasonable will depend on the type and circumstances of the job. Where an employee is hired on the basis of already having certain skills, it is not reasonable to expect the employer to provide training on those aspects; however, training may be required on company-specific procedures, tools or techniques.

Employees may be put on probation to allow a period within which their suitability for the job may be assessed. Even during a probation period, an employee should be given feedback on performance and appropriate evaluation, instruction, guidance, training and counselling to enable him to meet the required standards. There is no fixed period for probation; what is required is an assessment of how long is reasonably required to establish the suitability of the person for the position. Probation periods of three or six months are probably the most common.

4.3. Written Evaluations

Written evaluations of the employee's performance will be important in order for the employer to prove that it has complied with its obligations before contemplating dismissal for poor performance. In the absence of written documents, the employer will have great difficulty in showing that it has met the requirements. During the evaluation process, the parties should attempt to identify what issues are causing or hindering the employee's performance. The employee must also be made clearly aware of the performance standards that he is required to meet. The parties should agree on what action needs to be taken (by the employee and/or the employer) to remedy the problems. These goals should be written down and acknowledged by both parties and then monitored and reviewed on a regular basis. This may involve financial or other targets or the delivery of specific tasks.

Even where an employee is not under-performing, written performance evaluations are a useful tool against which the employee's progress can be tracked and which could be used by management for decision-making such as in the context of salary reviews, the award of performance bonuses and promotions. Performance may even be used as a criterion when considering the selection of employees for retrenchment, provided the evaluation was fair and objective. Evaluations should thus be conducted in an objective and fair manner, with employees being afforded the opportunity to comment on their evaluations. It may be desirable or even necessary to use an independent person to conduct the evaluation if it is being used to select employees for retrenchment. If tests are used, they should be recognized and reliable.

4.4. Warnings and Suspensions

The progressive disciplinary process envisages that warnings will be issued for most forms of misconduct (other than serious misconduct). There is no fixed rule as to how many warnings must be issued before dismissal, and formal procedures do not have to be invoked every time a rule is infringed. Minor transgressions may result in verbal rather than written warnings, which should nevertheless be recorded in the employee's personnel file. It is usual at some point to issue a final written warning which makes it clear to the employee that a further infraction will likely result in dismissal.

Warnings should generally state their period of validity. Again, there is no fixed rule for how long a warning may be valid; however, six months is generally and most widely used. Sometimes, final written warnings are made valid for longer periods, e.g., twelve months. Where the employer has specified the issue in its disciplinary code, these provisions should be followed, especially if the procedure has been agreed with the union.

There are two types of suspension, one is a form of disciplinary sanction, and the other is a precautionary measure pending an investigation and the finalization of disciplinary proceedings against an employee. In South Africa, suspension generally cannot be imposed as a sanction without the employee's consent (unless it is provided for in a collective agreement). Employees might consent to a period of suspension without pay as an alternative to dismissal if this is offered by the employer.

Precautionary suspension is used where an employee is reasonably suspected of serious misconduct but the investigation and disciplinary process is still in progress, and there are good reasons to exclude the employee from the workplace pending the outcome of the investigation and disciplinary process. The employee receives pay and benefits during the suspension period. The courts have held that employers need to act fairly towards employees in relation to suspensions, and must not hastily resort to suspending when circumstances do not warrant this course of action.[2] There must be a good reason to suspend, for example, because the employee could interfere with the investigation if not suspended, or because there is a real fear of ongoing harm or risk to the business (due, e.g., to the nature of the job and the suspected offence) or to another employee (e.g., in the case of assault or sexual harassment).

4.5. Checklist of Do's and Don'ts

- Set standards for conduct and performance to create certainty and consistency, and communicate these rules and standards in clear and simple terms. If they are too long-winded, your employees will not read them, and if they are complicated, there will be confusion about what is required.
- Decide on the form and content of rules that are appropriate to the nature and size of the business.
- Distinguish between misconduct and poor performance issues, so as to ensure that the correct process is used to deal with the problem.

2. *Premier of the Northwest Province & Another* (2009) 30 ILJ 605 (LC).

- Evaluate the performance of employees in a fair and objective manner and consider the employee's input. Respond to the employee if you disagree with his input.
- Ascertain the reasons for under-performance, and then set goals to overcome the problems.
- Do not issue formal disciplinary 'warnings' to an employee who is under-performing, as this does not indicate an attempt to find out and address the underlying cause of the under-performance. It also suggests that you are confusing performance issues with discipline.
- Always check what the company's internal procedures and codes require before taking action. Do not simply launch into action and then find afterwards that you bypassed your own procedures or requirements.
- Do not suspend employees in haste without considering whether such action is justified in the circumstances. The courts have been critical of employers for doing so.
- Do not impose suspension as a disciplinary sanction unless this is agreed (with the employee or because it is provided for in a collective agreement). Remember that employees might consent to a period of suspension without pay as an alternative to dismissal, if this is offered by the employer.

5. TERMINATION OF EMPLOYEES FOR PERFORMANCE OR DISCIPLINARY REASONS

5.1. Overview

The LRA requires that the termination of employment must be fair (which requires the employer to prove that there is a fair reason for the termination and to follow a fair termination procedure). Under the BCEA, the employer has to give minimum notice to the employee (except where summary dismissal is warranted) and make the relevant statutory termination payments. The minimum notice periods are one week if the employee has been employed for less than six months, two weeks if the employee has been employed for more than six months but less than one year, and four weeks if the employee has been employed for longer or is a farm or domestic worker who has been employed for more than six months. Unless the termination is a retrenchment (in which case statutory severance pay of at least one week's remuneration per completed year of service is payable), usually the only statutory payment due on termination is accrued annual leave pay.

Whether or not a dismissal for misconduct (which would be pursuant to a disciplinary process) or for poor performance (which would pursuant to a performance management process) is for a fair reason and follows a fair process is determined by the facts of the case.

Misconduct. Dismissal for misconduct is expected to be a measure of last resort, reserved for serious misconduct or for repeated misconduct where the employee has not heeded corrective disciplinary action such as warnings. The fundamental question to be asked (in deciding whether to dismiss) is whether the misconduct committed by the employee renders the continuation of the employment relationship intolerable. Generally, the courts accept that an employment relationship becomes objectively intolerable when the relationship of trust between employer and employee is irreparably destroyed. Examples of forms of misconduct that generally warrant dismissal include gross dishonesty, gross insubordination, wilfully endangering the safety of others, racism, and sexual harassment.

When deciding whether or not to dismiss an employee, the employer should consider, in addition to the gravity of the misconduct, factors such as the employee's circumstances (such as length of service, previous disciplinary record and personal circumstances), the nature of the job and the circumstances of the infringement itself. However, a clean disciplinary record and long service will not always assist an employee in avoiding dismissal. The courts have held that the only relevance of a clean record may be the extent to which it indicates that the employee is likely (or not) to repeat the offence and, where the employee shows no remorse and has, by his conduct, done nothing to show that he would not repeat his misconduct, there is no reason why the employer should have to show leniency. The essential question to be asked is whether the misconduct committed by the employee renders the continuation of the employment relationship objectively intolerable.

Procedurally, an employer is required to conduct an investigation into whether there are grounds for dismissal for misconduct. This does not need to be in the form of a formal disciplinary enquiry, but in practice, it usually is. The employee must be notified in advance of the allegations of misconduct against him/her using a form and language he/she can understand and he/she should be given the opportunity to state a case in response to the allegations. The employee is entitled to a reasonable time to prepare a response, and to the assistance of a trade union representative (where applicable) or a fellow employee to represent the employee in the process.

Where the employer has adopted a more procedurally onerous or complex disciplinary procedure (than the Code's guidelines), it will generally be bound to follow that procedure.

Poor performance. When the employee was aware or could reasonably have been expected to be aware of the required performance standard, and the employee was given a fair opportunity to meet the required performance standard but failed to do so, dismissal for performance is permissible. Dismissal must be the appropriate sanction for not meeting the required performance standard in the particular circumstances, and where the failure by an employee to meet a performance standard is for reasons beyond the employee's control, dismissal would not be justified.

A performance management process should be followed before dismissing for poor performance. The essential elements of such a process are dealt with in section 4 above. If the employee fails to improve after the reasonable time afforded to do so, a further meeting would be held with the employee at which to consider whether he should be dismissed for poor performance. The employee should be given an opportunity to state a case in this regard before deciding whether to dismiss.

Much of the above is covered in the Code.

As with employer-adopted disciplinary procedures, where the employer adopts a performance management procedure that is more onerous (than the Code's guidelines), it will generally be bound to follow that procedure.

Automatically unfair dismissals. An employee will be regarded as having been automatically unfairly dismissed where the reason for the dismissal is one of a limited list of reasons that are regarded as particularly unfair grounds for dismissal, and they include where the reason for the dismissal is that the employee participated in protected industrial action; a refusal by employees to accept a demand in respect of any matter of mutual interest between them and their employer; the employee exercised rights conferred by the LRA; the employee's pregnancy; unfair discrimination against an employee, a transfer of a business as a going concern; or victimization of a whistleblower.

Separation/Severance Pay. An employee whose employment is fairly terminated for misconduct or poor performance is not entitled to any separation or severance pay. Dismissal for misconduct will generally be summary (i.e., without notice) while dismissal for poor performance will be on notice. On termination, in either event, the employer only has to pay accrued entitlements to remuneration for time already worked and accrued annual leave pay.

If, however, the employee is dismissed due to the employer's operational requirements (e.g., where the employee's position has become redundant due to lack of work or the introduction of new technology), the employee must be paid severance pay of at least the equivalent of one week's remuneration for each completed year of continuous service with the employer, unless the employee unreasonably refuses an offer of alternative employment, in which case no severance pay is payable.

Under a separation or settlement agreement with a departing employee, the employer may agree to compensate the employee with additional payments or benefits in exchange for a full and final settlement of any claims that the employee may have against the employer.

An employer is obliged to notify the Department of Home Affairs of the termination of a foreign work visa holder's services for any reason.

5.2. Fines and Penalties

Arbitrators and courts must order reinstatement or re-employment of an unfairly dismissed employee unless the dismissed employee does not wish to return to the employer, the arbitrator or court is satisfied that the resumption of the employment relationship would be intolerable or impracticable or where the dismissal was only procedurally unfair. If reinstatement is ordered, the employer may be required to pay the employee's wages from the date of dismissal to the date of the reinstatement order (i.e., back pay), which can be a period of years depending on the court process.

If reinstatement or re-employment is not awarded, unfairly dismissed employees may be granted financial compensation. Where the dismissal is found to be unfair either because the employer did not prove that the reason for the dismissal was fair or the employer did not follow a fair procedure (or both), the compensation awarded must be just and equitable in all the circumstances, but may not be more than the equivalent of twelve months' remuneration. In the case of automatically unfair dismissals, the maximum is double that of other unfair dismissals, that is, twenty-four months' remuneration.

Employees are subject to sanctions for contravention or non-compliance with their duties and obligations in relation to foreign workers under the Immigration Act. Stricter compliance is required of employers with more than five employees or who have prior convictions under the Immigration Act.

5.3. Checklist of Do's and Don'ts

Before dismissing an employee for disciplinary reasons, check that the answers to the following questions are 'yes' to ensure that the dismissal will be for a fair reason:

(1) Did the employee contravene a rule or standard regulating conduct in or of relevance to the workplace? Identify what the rule/standard is and whether it was contravened. In some cases, identifying the rule is easy (e.g., employees must not steal) but proving the contravention is not, while in other cases it is harder to identify the rule (e.g., where

there is a breach of company procedures, but the procedures are derived from a practice, not a written policy).

(2) If a rule or standard was contravened:
   - Was the rule valid or reasonable? Assess this on a rule by rule basis (in most instances this should not be a problem);
   - Was the employee aware or could he/she reasonably be expected to be aware of the rule or standard? For obvious rules (e.g., employees must not steal), this will be easy. For less obvious rules (e.g., procedural rules specific to a workplace), check that the rules were communicated in policy manuals, written instructions, etc.;
   - Has the rule or standard been consistently been applied by the employer? Check that the rule applies to all employees in similar positions and that those who similarly contravened were also dismissed. Where an employee was previously not dismissed for similar misconduct, check for legitimate distinguishing features;
   - Is dismissal an appropriate sanction for the contravention? Only cases of serious misconduct or a repeated transgression committed despite disciplinary warnings will warrant dismissal as a sanction.

Before dismissing an employee for poor performance, check that the answers to the following questions are ‘yes’ to ensure that the dismissal will be for a fair reason:

- Did the employee fail to meet a performance standard?

  If so:

- Was the employee aware or could he reasonably be expected to be aware of the required performance standard?
- Was the employee given a fair opportunity to meet the required performance standard? The period of time afforded to the employee must have entailed a reasonable time within which the employee could raise his performance to the required standard.
- Is dismissal an appropriate sanction for not meeting the required performance standard? Only resort to dismissal if there are no other ways of remedying the problem of poor performance (e.g., training, adapting duties, etc.).

6. LAYOFFS, REDUCTIONS IN FORCE, AND/OR REDUNDANCIES AS A RESULT OF JOB ELIMINATIONS OR OTHER RESTRUCTURING

6.1. Overview

An employee may be dismissed for a reason relating to the operational requirements of the employer. Operational requirements are defined in section 213 of the LRA as requirements based on the employer's economic, technological, structural or similar needs. This usually arises where the employer closes its operations, downsizes or restructures its business activities.

A dismissal based on operational requirements must be both procedurally and substantively fair. The employer must be able to show an objectively established operational or business rationale for the decision which will lead to job losses. If the decision to retrench is not shown to make rational, business sense, the dismissal could be set aside by an arbitrator or the Labour Court. While arbitrators and Courts are slow to interfere with the employer's prerogative to run the business as it sees fit, and they have held that it is fair to retrench when the business is financially sound but wishes to become more profitable,[3] the business case must be bona fide and objective and the retrenchments should be proportional to the business advantage to be achieved.

6.2. Reductions in Force/Layoffs/Job Eliminations

A lay-off is often used to refer to a temporary period during which an employee's services are not required, and they are not paid, but where their employment is not terminated. In South Africa an employer may not unilaterally lay-off employees for a temporary period, rather this must be done by agreement after consultation with the employee. Layoffs are usually a means to avoid dismissals for operational reasons (retrenchments). Sometimes temporary lay-off procedures form part of collective agreements concluded in bargaining councils that are applicable to industry.

The process that must be followed when considering retrenchments is set forth in section 189 or 189A of the LRA. The basic section 189 provisions apply to all retrenchments, and section 189A imposes additional requirements and prescribes different procedures for disputes where large businesses conduct large-scale retrenchments. An employer is a large employer if it employs fifty or more employees. A retrenchment is identified

3. *See*, e.g., *Mazista Tiles (Pty) Ltd. v. NUM* 2004 (25) ILJ 2156 (LAC); *Greyvenstein v. Flaming Silver Trading 62 (Pty) Ltd. t/a Sunglass World* 2007 (28) ILJ 1081 (LC).

as large or small-scale depending on the number of employees to be retrenched with reference both to the current retrenchment and to any employees retrenched in the preceding twelve months. The threshold is roughly 10% of the workforce, but the specific scale works as follows:

Number of Employees Contemplated to be Retrenched	*Total Number of Employees*
At least 10	Up to 200
At least 20	201–300
At least 30	301–400
At least 40	401–500
At least 50	More than 500

Section 189 requires consultation with the employees who may potentially be dismissed, or their representatives, on the proposed retrenchments. The employer must discuss ways to avoid entrenchment with the first body on the following list that applies to it:

- any person (or body, such as a trade union) with whom it is required to consult pursuant to a collective agreement; or
- a workplace forum, if there is one which applies to the workplace where the employees it proposes retrenching work, and any registered trade union whose members are likely to be affected by the proposed retrenchments; or
- any registered trade union whose members are likely to be affected by the proposed retrenchments; or
- the employees likely to be affected or their representatives, nominated for that purpose. If none of the first three apply, employers must consult with the employees themselves.

The employer must start consulting when it contemplates retrenching. The Labour Court has stated this means when retrenchments are reasonably foreseeable.[4] The discussion can include ways to avoid retrenchments or keep the number of retrenchments as low as possible, opportunities to change the timing of retrenchments in order to mitigate the hardships caused to employees who are retrenched, how to select the employees to be retrenched, and what is to be paid to retrenched employees (severance pay).

Consultation must commence with the employer issuing a written notice inviting the other party to consult and disclosing relevant information to enable the other consulting party to engage in the consultation process.

4. *See SATAWU v. Old Mutual Life Assurance Co. of S. Afr. Ltd.* 2005 BLLR 378 (LC).

Section 189(3) of the LRA provides that the notice must, at a minimum, cover the following:

- the reasons for the proposed retrenchments;
- the alternatives the employer considered before proposing retrenchment, and the reasons for rejecting each of those alternatives;
- the number of employees likely to be affected, and the job categories in which they are employed;
- the selection criteria the employer proposes using to select which employees to retrench;
- when retrenchments are likely to take effect (a specific date or a period of time);
- the severance pay proposed for retrenched employees;
- any assistance that can be offered to employees likely to be retrenched;
- the possibility of future re-employment of retrenched employees;
- the number of employees employed by the employer; and
- the number of employees the employer has retrenched in the last twelve months (the last two are included so that the employees or their representatives can identify whether a large-scale retrenchment is applicable and whether section 189A procedures should be followed).

There is no fixed rule in ordinary (small-scale) retrenchments as to how long the consultation must take place, but there must be proper consultation and canvassing of all the relevant issues. The LRA says that consultation must be meaningful.[5] The parties must work together to attempt to reach consensus.[6] The courts have regularly said that sham consultations are insufficient.[7]

If the union or the employees make representations during the process, the employer must respond to them and must state reasons for disagreeing, if applicable. If representations are made in writing, the employer must respond in writing.

Facilitation is an additional (voluntary) process available to the parties to a large-scale retrenchment on request. It involves a request to the CCMA and the appointment of a CCMA commissioner to act as the facilitator, who will meet with the parties at least four times in an attempt to help them come to an agreement on the retrenchments. Facilitation occurs simultaneously with the normal consultation process. Either party can request the CCMA to appoint a facilitator provided that the union must represent the majority of employees before it is entitled to do so. If the employer wants to request facilitation, it must be done at the same time as initiating a consultation with the union/employees – i.e., when the section 189(3) notice inviting

5. Section 189(2).
6. Section 189(2).
7. *See*, e.g., *Robinson v. PriceWaterhouseCoopers* 2006 (27) ILJ 836 (LC).

consultation over proposed retrenchments is issued. If the employer has not applied for facilitation and the union/employees want to do so, they have fifteen days after receiving the section 189(3) notice in which to do so.

If a facilitator is appointed, then the employer may not give notice of dismissal until sixty days have elapsed from the date on which the section 189(3) notice has been sent, but a consulting party (such as the employer) may not unreasonably refuse to extend this period for consultation if an extension is required to ensure meaningful consultation. The period of notice given must be the statutory minimum or the contractual notice period, if longer. An employer may elect to pay in lieu of giving notice.

If a facilitator is not appointed, a party cannot refer a dispute (about the retrenchments) to a council or the CCMA unless thirty days have elapsed from the date on which the section 189(3) notice has been given. (Such a dispute referral would ensure that at least a conciliation hearing takes place where a CCMA commissioner can attempt to mediate the dispute.) Thereafter, a further thirty days must elapse or a certificate indicating that the dispute has not been resolved must be issued by the CCMA before notice of termination can be given. Practically, this usually amounts to a sixty-day period.

Some Bargaining Council Agreements require that notice of any retrenchments also be given to the Bargaining Council. The agreement will provide what form the notice must take, and when it must be given.

As part of its duty to avoid retrenchment, wherever possible, the employer must explore alternatives to retrenchment. Where the employer has work that an existing employee can do (even if some training is required), then the employer should accommodate the existing employee. The employer must also consult about the method of selecting employees to be retrenched, and in the absence of agreed criteria must adopt fair and objective criteria (last-in-first-out is often used, sometimes subject to some qualifications).

There are statutory rights to severance pay for retrenched employees. An employer must pay an employee dismissed for operational requirements severance pay equal to at least one week's remuneration for each completed year of continuous service with that employer. Remuneration for purposes of the severance pay calculation generally means any payment in cash or in kind made or owing to the employee in return for the employee working for the employer. Specific types of payments that are to be included and excluded from remuneration in this regard are regulated in a Ministerial notice, particularly government Notice 691 of 23 May 2003. The employer and employee can agree on a higher amount of severance pay. Employees who unreasonably refuse offers of alternative employment with the retrenching employer, or any other employer, are not entitled to severance pay. Reasonableness is judged on the facts of the case, so there is no universal standard that can be explained.

The employer usually agrees to re-hire retrenched employees if business increases, or if it later considers hiring people for the work that the retrenched employee performed and this is an issue on which it must consult. Usually, the parties agree on a time period during which the re-hiring arrangement will apply, and make it subject to the employer being able to contact the employee.

Employers may conclude settlement agreements with retrenched employees that include a release of claims against the employer. To ensure that such a settlement is valid and binding, the employees must understand the terms of the agreement and acknowledge that they are giving up potential claims. The parties must conclude the agreement voluntarily and without duress.

6.3. Fines and Penalties

There are no fines for breach of the LRA retrenchment requirements. However, employees who believe they have been unfairly retrenched can refer a dispute to the Labour Court, after first referring it to the CCMA for conciliation (where the retrenchment process involved a single employee, or the employer is a small employer (i.e., employing less than ten employees), the employee(s) can also choose to refer an unfair dismissal dispute to arbitration at the CCMA instead of to the Labour Court). If the retrenchments are found to be substantively unfair, the employees can be reinstated or be awarded compensation of up to twelve months' remuneration. If the retrenchments were only procedurally unfair, then the court can only award compensation.

In large-scale retrenchments, employees who dispute the fairness of the procedure must file an urgent application with the Labour Court. The Court has wide powers to intervene in the dispute, including the power to order the employer to comply with procedural requirements and to issue an injunction against dismissals pending compliance with the statutory procedure. Where the employees dispute the fairness of the reasons for the retrenchments, they have the option of either embarking on a strike over the issue (usually strikes over the fairness of a dismissal are not permitted because such disputes are subject to adjudication or arbitration, but there is an exception to this for large-scale retrenchments) or requesting the Labour Court to adjudicate the dispute.

6.4. Checklist of Do's and Don'ts

- Record facts and figures to substantiate sound, objective business reasons for any proposal to reduce the workforce and do not start consulting until you are sure that your business case makes sense.
- Identify the correct body with whom to consult and start consulting as soon as retrenchments are contemplated/reasonably foreseeable. Do not make the mistake of consulting only with one union when members of another union are affected, even if it is the majority union (unless this is prescribed in a collective agreement).
- Prepare a section 189(3) notice disclosing all the required information because if you do not provide information to back up your proposal the union is likely to delay the process by asking for information and refusing to consult until it is supplied. The Courts have said a union is entitled to do this.
- Respond to any queries raised by employees or their representatives, giving an explanation (in writing) if you reject their proposals, and keep accurate minutes of meetings held with the unions/employees and circulate the minutes to them soon after the meeting.
- Carefully record any agreement reached with employees in writing to avoid possible disputes at a later stage.
- Do not allow subjective views to influence the process of selecting employees to be retrenched.
- Do not refuse requests for information unless the information is irrelevant or confidential.
- Where confidentiality is an issue, make an arrangement to disclose information subject to a duty to keep it confidential or withhold only the sensitive information, rather than refusing to disclose at all.
- Do not give notice of retrenchment before the minimum time period for a consultation has run out (in large-scale retrenchments) or before there has been a proper consultation on all the issues.
- If you are concluding a settlement agreement with employees to be retrenched, make sure the employees understand exactly what they are agreeing to and what rights they are giving up. You can do this by suggesting that they take legal advice before signing and by recording this in the settlement agreement.

7. LABOUR AND EMPLOYMENT LAW RAMIFICATIONS UPON ACQUISITION OR SALE OF A BUSINESS

7.1. Overview

Section 197 of the LRA regulates the transfer of a business as a going concern from one employer to another. If the sale is achieved by a sale of shares section 197 does not apply. The employees remain employed by the entity, and the shares simply transfer from the seller to the buyer. From the point of view of sound industrial relations, it is a good idea to communicate effectively with employees about a sale of the shares in a business even though there is no legal obligation to do so, to avoid unnecessary uncertainty, fears and disputes. The real issues arise, however, in the context of the sale of a business as a going concern.

Work visas are usually both employer and position specific, and regard must thus be had to whether it is necessary to procure new work visas for staff members who hold work visas.

7.2. Acquisition of a Business

The effect of section 197 is that, unless otherwise agreed (with the affected employees), the acquiring employer is automatically substituted in the place of the selling employer with respect to all contracts of employment in existence immediately before the date of transfer. All rights and obligations between the selling employer and an employee at the time of the transfer continue in force as if they had been rights and obligations between the acquiring employer and the employee. The acquiring employer thus automatically becomes the employer of all the employees employed in the transferring business.

The transfer does not interrupt the employees' continuity of employment. Anything done before the transfer by or in relation to the selling employer, including the dismissal of an employee, the commission of an unfair labour practice or an act of unfair discrimination is considered to have been done by or in relation to the acquiring employer.

The transfer of the employees from the selling employer to the acquiring employer happens automatically by operation of law. The employees do not have the right to object to the transfer nor do they become entitled to any severance pay.

Furthermore, section 197 requires that employees transfer either on the same terms and conditions of employment or on terms and conditions of employment that are (different but) on the whole not less favourable. This does not prevent the acquiring employer from transferring employees to a different pension, provident or similar fund, provided the provisions of section 14(1)(c) of the Pension Funds Act No. 25 of 1956 are complied with. The Pension Funds Registrar must be satisfied that any scheme to amalgamate or transfer funds is reasonable and equitable, and accords full recognition to the rights and reasonable benefit expectations of the persons concerned in terms of the pension fund rules, and to the additional benefits which have become an established practice.

Where the employees' conditions of employment are determined by a collective agreement, the acquiring employer must comply with the conditions of employment in the collective agreement, that is, the acquiring employer does not have the flexibility to offer different but 'on the whole not less favourable' terms and conditions.

It is possible to avoid the consequences of section 197 (such as the automatic transfer of all employees on their existing terms and conditions) by agreement, but such agreements must comply with the provisions of section 197(6). Thus, the agreement must be in writing and concluded between the selling employer, the acquiring employer or the selling and acquiring employers acting jointly, on the one hand, and the appropriate body or persons referred to in section 189 of the LRA, on the other hand (i.e., the same entity as the employer is obliged to consult if considering retrenchments). This means that employer parties cannot reach agreement on these matters without the employees' consent obtained either via their authorized representative or from each individual employee directly.

The selling and acquiring employers must agree on the value of certain entitlements for transferring employees (e.g., accrued leave and the contingent liability for severance pay) and agree which of them is liable for these amounts. The terms of this agreement must be disclosed to each transferring employee. In practice, this is done either as part of the sale of a business agreement or, more frequently, as a separate agreement annexed to the sale of business agreement (which can then be more easily disclosed to employees). Moreover, the selling employer must also take other reasonable measures to ensure that adequate provision is made for any obligation the acquiring employer assumed. The LRA does not specify what sort of measures are required, but in practice this has involved, for example, transferring the required funds into an attorney's trust account for safe-keeping until such time as the payments must be made.

7.3. Acquisition Checklist

The acquiring employer should conduct due diligence on the employees it will inherit with the business, and the obligations it will assume. The acquiring employer should consider the financial ramifications of the obligations for which it will be responsible, and make sure that they are reflected in the purchase price. Where appropriate, warranties should be sought from the selling employer. The acquiring employer will also need to consider whether it will be able to match the existing terms and conditions of employment or provide others that are on the whole no less favourable. Specifically, the acquiring employer should request:

- details of all employees on the payroll who would transfer with the business, their length of service and their current remuneration package;
- calculation of the accrued rights each transferring employee is likely to have as of the date of transfer (e.g., accrued leave and bonuses earned but not yet paid out);
- a description of the retirement fund and medical aid scheme/health insurance plan currently available to employees (if any), what contributions are paid and by whom and what benefits the plan provides;
- a list of any unusual or extraordinary contractual provisions applicable to employees (e.g., unusually long notice periods, unusual benefits or allowances or other departures from standard terms and conditions);
- a list of any current disputes with existing employees;
- confirmation of compliance with all relevant labour legislation and that any required levies are up-to-date (such as unemployment insurance, COIDA and Employment Equity reports).
- consider whether new work visas are required or whether work visas require amendment.

7.4. Sale of a Business

Unless the selling employer is able to show that it complied with its obligations under section 197, it will be jointly and severally liable for certain entitlements (such as accrued leave and severance pay calculated to the date of transfer) payable to transferred employees who are retrenched or who lose their employment through the insolvency of the acquiring employer within twelve months of the transfer. The selling employer must also take reasonable measures to ensure that adequate provision is made for any obligation the acquiring employer assumes for the transferring employee entitlements described above.

The selling employer may also need to consider a reduction in the selling price it seeks for its business in light of the nature and extent of the obligations taken over by the acquiring employer. In some instances, the parties may agree that some obligations are retained by the selling employer (e.g., a pro rata payment towards severance benefits in the event of a retrenchment within a stipulated period of time).

7.5. Sale of a Business Checklist

- Ensure that the acquiring employer has made adequate provision for the accrued liabilities towards employees that it is taking over.
- Provide for an indemnity from the acquiring employer in the event that it fails to fulfil its obligations and where the selling employer may be sued by disgruntled employees.
- Consider whether the selling employer needs to amend the purchase price in light of the various obligations taken over by the acquiring employer.
- The sale of a business may impact the suitability of the work visas held by existing foreign national employees and are likely to necessitate applications for new work visas.

8. USE OF ALTERNATIVE WORKFORCES: INDEPENDENT CONTRACTORS, CONTRACT EMPLOYEES, AND TEMPORARY OR LEASED WORKERS

8.1. Overview

The use of alternative workforces, whether in the form of independent contractors, fixed-term and part-time contract employees or workers from temporary employment services or agencies (commonly referred to in South Africa as labour brokers), has historically been commonplace among South African employers. Such workforces were often used as a means to address fluctuating labour requirements, but in many instances, it was a way of reducing labour costs (in that it usually costs less to employ such employees).

The use of alternative workforces is permissible under the LRA and the BCEA, but since 1 January 2015, it has become subject to fairly extensive regulation, via legislative amendments aimed at substantially limiting the scope for the use of labour brokers and fixed-term contract employees and better protecting these employees (and part-time employees). Details of this regulation are dealt with below.

After a moratorium by the Department of Home Affairs on the issuance of work visas to labour brokers or temporary employment services or agencies which lasted many years, the Department of Home Affairs currently does issue work visas to foreign employees rendering services to such agencies.

8.2. Independent Contractors

8.2.1. Definition

There is no statutory definition of an independent contractor. The historical approach of the courts was to consider whether the dominant impression or reality of the relationship was one of employment or one as between a client and an independent contractor, and various factors were identified as indicators either way. In a judgment on the issue,[8] the LAC identified three 'primary' criteria for the determination of the question of whether a relationship was one of employment (or independent contractor), namely: (1) whether there is an employer's right to supervision and control; (2) whether the employee forms an integral party of the organization with the employer; and (3) the extent to which the employee is economically dependent upon the employer.

Applying these criteria to distinguish an independent contractor from an employee involves a factual analysis of the reality of the relationship in relation to each criterion, and the fact that the parties may label a person an independent contractor in the contract, for example, does not necessarily mean that the person will be regarded as such.

The more vulnerable and low skilled the person, the more likely it is that he/she will be regarded as an employee and not an independent contractor. For example, for a person earning below the BCEA earnings threshold,[9] the LRA and the BCEA establish a rebuttable presumption that an employment relationship exists if one or more of the following factors are present:

- the manner in which the person works is subject to the control or direction of the other person;
- the person's hours of work are subject to the control or direction of the other person;
- in the case of a person who works for an organization, the person forms part of that organization;
- the person has worked for that other person for an average of at least forty hours per month over the last three months;
- the person is economically dependent on the other person for whom he/she works or renders services;
- the person is provided with tools of trade or work equipment by the other person; or
- the person only works for or renders services to one person.

8. *State Information Technology Agency (Pty) Ltd v. Commission for Conciliation Mediation and Arbitration and Others* (2008) 29 ILJ 2234 (LAC).
9. *See supra* n. 1.

The LRA's Code of Good Practice: Who Is an Employee also provides guidance in the determination of when a person is an independent contractor. For example, it lists six factors to distinguish an employee from an independent contractor:

- an employee is contracted to render personal services whereas an independent contractor is contracted to perform specified work or produce a specified result;
- an employee must perform services personally whereas an independent contractor may usually perform through others;
- an employer may choose when to make use of the services of an employee whereas an independent contractor must perform work or produce a result within a period fixed by contract;
- an employee is obliged to perform the lawful commands and instructions of the employer while the independent contractor is subservient to the contract and is not under the supervision or control of the employer;
- an employee's contract terminates on his or her death while this is not necessarily the case with an independent contractor;
- an employee's contract terminates on the expiry of a period of service while an independent contractor's contract terminates on completion of the specified work or the achievement of the specified result for which he or she was contracted.

With effect from 1 January 2015, an amendment to the LRA (section 200B) was also introduced aimed at dealing with artificial arrangements that may be used by some to avoid employment obligations. Under the amendment, for purposes of the LRA and any other employment law, the term 'employer' includes one or more persons who carry on an associated or related activity or business by or through an employer if the intent or effect of their doing so is or has been to directly or indirectly defeat the purposes of the LRA or any other employment law. If more than one person is held to be the employer of an employee in terms of section 200B, those persons are jointly and severally liable for any failure to comply with the obligations of an employer in terms of the LRA or any other employment law. The scope for applying this amendment in practice remains to be seen.

It is important to bear in mind that none of the available mainstream work visa categories are available to foreign independent contractors, as these are usually based upon an employment relationship. Various embassies have expressed reticence to issue business visitor's visas to independent contractors wanting to render temporary services in South Africa, although some embassies will readily do so.

8.2.2. Creating the Relationship

Although a written contract is not legally required to establish a relationship with an independent contractor, it is advisable to minimize the scope for disputes. The contract should reflect the reality of the relationship and particularly the fact that the contractor is obliged to produce a specified result, as opposed to just making available his/her productive capacity. The contract should state that the person is an independent contractor and not an employee, record that the person is free to do work for and earn income from others, and it should not provide for the sorts of arrangements described above as indicators of employment (e.g., providing tools of the trade, controlling the person's hours of work and the manner in which he works).

8.2.3. Compensation

The compensation payable to an independent contractor should be linked, where possible, to the production of results by him under the contract. Compensation that is linked to time spent runs the risk of being an indicator of an employment relationship. If an independent contractor is afforded employment-type benefits, such as leave, staff discounts, etc., this will tend to indicate that he is, in fact, an employee. A person who is a true independent contractor is not entitled to any employment benefits, minimum wages or annual leave. The independent contractor is responsible for paying wages and benefits of its own employees.

8.2.4. Other Terms and Conditions

A contract with an independent contractor should provide clearly for its commencement and duration, the rendering of invoices (where appropriate) for payment purposes, the assumption of risk and appropriate indemnities in respect of the work performed by the independent contractor and the arrangements for any access provided to the client's facilities and property. If the independent contractor is going to be in control of part of the company's premises for the duration of the work (e.g., where the contractor is constructing something on site), written arrangements should be concluded with the contractor in accordance with the relevant occupational health and safety legislation (such as OHSA) which puts responsibility for health and safety in the area in question on the independent contractor.

8.3. Contract Workers

In most instances, the term 'contract workers' is used to refer to persons who are engaged by an employer on a temporary, fixed-term or casual basis. The nature of the relationship is usually one of employment but for a fixed term (as opposed to an indefinite or 'permanent' relationship). Fixed-term employment contracts are permissible in law, but on 1 January 2015 significant restrictions were introduced regulating such contracts for employees earning below the BCEA earnings threshold. For employees earning above the threshold or where the employer is a small employer (employing less than ten employees) or a slightly larger but new employer (employing less than fifty employees and in operation for less than two years, unless the employer conducts multiple businesses or was formed by the dissolution of an existing business), the regulations do not apply.

For employees to whom the restrictions introduced in 2015 apply:

- Employers may only employ such employees on fixed-term contracts (or successive fixed-term contracts) for longer than three months if the nature of the work for which the employees are engaged is of limited or definite duration, or the employer can demonstrate any other justifiable reason for fixing the term of the contract. Employment in terms of a fixed-term contract concluded or renewed contrary to the above is deemed to be indefinite employment.
- A non-exhaustive list of nine 'justifiable reasons' for fixing the term of a contract is specified, that is where the employee (1) is replacing another employee who is temporarily absent from work; (2) is engaged on account of a temporary increase in the volume of work which is not expected to endure beyond twelve months; (3) is a student or recent graduate who is employed for the purpose of being trained or gaining work experience; (4) is employed to work exclusively on a specific project; (5) is a non-citizen who has been granted a work permit for a defined period; (6) is engaged to perform seasonal work; (7) is employed in an official public works scheme or similar public job creation scheme; (8) is engaged in a position which is funded by an external source for a limited period; (9) or has reached the normal or agreed retirement age applicable in the employer's business.
- An offer of a fixed-term contract must be in writing and must state the reason for the fixed term of the contract.
- Employees employed on fixed-term contracts of more than three months (even where this is for a justifiable reason) must be treated no less favourably than an employee on an indefinite contract performing the same or similar work unless there is a justifiable reason for treating the employee differently. Justifiable reasons for treating such a fixed-term

employee differently are stipulated to include seniority, experience or length of service; merit; the quality or quantity of work performed; or any other criteria of a similar nature that is not unfairly discriminatory.

- An employee on any fixed-term contract must be provided with the same access to opportunities to apply for vacancies as are provided to employees employed by the employer on an indefinite basis.
- Where the fixed-term contract is for longer than twenty-four months, severance pay of one week's remuneration per completed year of the contract is payable on the expiry of the contract.

For employees to whom the 2015 regulations do not apply, the fixed term of the contract may be linked to time (i.e., it can provide that it lapses on a specified termination date) or to the happening of a specific event (such as the completion of a task). Where the parties have agreed that the contract will terminate on the occurrence of a particular event or the completion of a particular task, the onus will generally rest on the employer to prove that the event has occurred or the task was in fact completed.

Unless otherwise agreed upon (e.g., through the inclusion of termination on notice provision in the contract), a fixed-term contract cannot be terminated prior to the end of the term without good cause for summary termination and a fair procedure being followed.

If an employee's fixed-term contract of employment (that has not become indefinite under the 2015 regulations referred above) expires without the employee having a reasonable expectation of its renewal or of being retained in employment on an indefinite basis, the expiry of the contract will not amount to a dismissal under the LRA and therefore the employer will not have to prove that it was for a fair reason or that it followed a fair procedure. If there was a reasonable expectation of its renewal of the employee being retained in employment on an indefinite basis, however, the non-renewal or non-appointment will amount to a dismissal which must then be shown by the employer to be fair.

Part-time workers earning below the threshold (unless they are employed by an employer who is a small employer or a slightly larger but new employer, or they work less than twenty-four hours per month) also enjoy some specific protections under the LRA. After three months of employment, they must be treated on the whole not less favourably than an employee doing comparable full-time work unless there is a justifiable reason for treating the employee differently, which includes similar access to training and skills development.

8.4. Leased Workers

Leased workers are generally provided to businesses by what is described in South African employment legislation as temporary employment services (more commonly referred to as labour brokers). The supply of leased workers will constitute a labour broking arrangement if the labour broker, for reward, provides the client with other persons who perform work for the client but who are remunerated by the labour broker.

The provision of leased workers is permissible in law but, as was the case with fixed-term contract employees, on 1 January 2015 significant restrictions were introduced regulating the supply of leased workers earning below the BCEA earnings threshold. For such employees:

- Only if the worker is performing a 'temporary service' is the labour broker deemed to be the employer of the worker. 'Temporary service' is limited to instances where the worker works for the client for a period not exceeding three months or replaces a temporarily absent employee of the client or the work falls in a category of work that is determined to be 'temporary service' under a Bargaining Council Agreement or a Ministerial determination.
- If the worker is not performing a 'temporary service', the client is deemed to be the employer of the worker for the purposes of the LRA (and to the exclusion of the labour broker)[10] and the worker's employment is deemed to be indefinite unless it is a legitimate fixed-term contract in accordance with the fixed-term contract restrictions described in section 8.3 above. In addition, the worker is then also entitled to be treated on the whole not less favourably than an employee of the client performing the same or similar work, unless there is a 'justifiable reason' for different treatment (justifiable reasons have the same meaning described in section 8.3 above, that is seniority, experience or length of service; merit; the quality or quantity of work performed; or any other criteria of a similar nature that is not unfairly discriminatory).

Aside from the above specific arrangements for workers earning below the BCEA earnings threshold, for labour broking arrangements generally:

- The labour broker is deemed (by express provisions in the LRA and the BCEA) to be the employer of the leased workers.
- The labour broker must provide the leased worker with written particulars of employment as required by the BCEA.

10. The Constitutional Court has indicated that, while the client's deemed the exclusive employer for purposes of the LRA, the labour broker could still play a role as an employer of the employee for purposes of other employment law (*Assign Services (Pty) Ltd v. National Union of Metalworkers of South Africa and others* [2018] 9 BLLR 837 (CC).

- A leased worker's terms and conditions must comply with any Bargaining Council Agreement or sectoral determination applicable to the industry in which the client (as opposed to the labour broker) is engaged.
- The labour broker must be registered in terms of the Employment Services Act.
- A leased worker who is a true independent contractor to the labour broker is not the employee of the labour broker, despite the deeming provisions.
- Although the labour broker is the employer of the leased workers, the client is jointly and severally liable with the broker to the leased workers for any contraventions by the labour broker of the BCEA or other wage regulating measures (such as applicable collective agreements).
- Trade unions seeking to exercise organizational rights in respect of leased workers are entitled to exercise those rights either in a workplace of the labour broker or in a workplace of one or more clients of the labour broker.

Where the leased workers are not deemed to be the client's employees, the client does not enjoy the COIDA immunity from liability to them for injuries and deaths in the workplace (*see* section 12 below regarding the COIDA immunity).

It is important to bear in mind that none of the available mainstream work visa categories are available to leased workers, as these usually require an employment relationship.

8.5. Checklist of Do's and Don'ts

- Before entering into arrangements using alternative workforces, carefully consider the true nature of the relationship and then contract for that relationship.
- When contracting with an independent contractor, make sure you contract for the delivery of a result and not his productive capacity and do not provide him with employment-type benefits.
- Check whether the workers to be used under the alternative workforce arrangements qualify for the special protections (e.g., those earning under the BCEA threshold) and, if they do, consider if it still makes sense to use them on that basis (e.g., if they will be deemed to be your employees, or you become obliged to treat them no less favourably than your permanent employees, ask yourself if there is still an advantage in contracting with them on the alternative basis. If it does still make sense, make sure the contracts applicable to them comply with the legislated requirements.
- In fixed-term employment contracts, make it clear when the contract will expire (refer to a specific date or an objectively ascertainable event), state

the reason why it is for a fixed term (for employees earning below the BCEA threshold) and do not provide for or say anything that will give the employee a reasonable expectation of the renewal of the contract or permanent employment if you do not want to have to justify the fairness of the expiry of the contract. For example, do not say that the contract may be renewed if the employee performs well.

– Do not simply sign the labour broking contract prepared by a labour broker. Get your own contract prepared that clearly regulates all aspects of the relationship, including in it flexibility in relation to the workers supplied, indemnities from the broker in relation to contraventions of minimum benefits obligations and termination provisions.

9. OBLIGATION TO BARGAIN COLLECTIVELY WITH TRADE UNIONS: RIGHT TO STRIKE AND A COMPANY'S RIGHT TO CONTINUE BUSINESS OPERATIONS

9.1. Overview of Unions' Right to Organize

Trade unions enjoy constitutional rights to determine their own administration and activities, to organize and to form and join a trade union federation, and they also have a constitutional right to engage in collective bargaining.

The LRA regulates how unions may exercise these organizational rights and, importantly, it does not impose a statutory duty on employers to bargain with unions over wages and terms and conditions, instead of leaving the securing of such obligations to the bargaining power of the unions. Unions that achieve certain representation in a workplace can win basic statutory organizational rights, such as access to the workplace to recruit members, stop orders for union dues and time off for union office bearers (the union must be 'sufficiently representative' to get these rights, which usually means that about 25% of the employees must be members). Rights to the appointment of shop stewards and leave for shop stewards training require majority representation on the union's part. *See* section 9.3 below for further information in this regard. The more substantive matter of bargaining on wages can only be secured by agreement with the employer.

Unions and their members can embark on lawful strike action to compel employers to agree to the union's demands about matters of mutual interest provided that they comply with the LRA's requirements for protected strikes. Employers have a similar right to resort to a lockout to compel a union and its members to agree to the employer's demands. The general procedural requirements entail the following:

- the issue in dispute must be referred by a party to the CCMA or a bargaining council with jurisdiction if there is one for the industry in question;
- the CCMA or a bargaining council with jurisdiction will then convene a conciliation meeting between the parties at which it will attempt to facilitate a settlement of the dispute;
- if the dispute is not settled, a certificate of non-resolution will be issued by the CCMA or a bargaining council with jurisdiction and, once this happens, either the employer or the employees can give forty-eight hours' written notice of commencement of the strike or lockout.

There are restrictions, however, in relation to the permissible subject matter of a strike or lockout. The general point of departure is that parties may strike or lockout over any matter of mutual interest unless it falls within one of the categories of issues or instances where strikes and lockouts are prohibited, namely:

- where the party is bound by a collective agreement that prohibits a strike or lockout over the issue in dispute;
- where the party is bound by an agreement that requires the issue in dispute to be referred to arbitration;
- where the issue in dispute is one that a party has a right to refer to arbitration or to the Labour Court pursuant to the LRA;
- where the party is engaged in an essential service or a maintenance service; or
- where, subject to a collective agreement, the party is bound by any arbitration award or collective agreement that regulates the issue in dispute, or certain determinations made under the LRA.

Unions, employees and employers taking part in a strike or lockout that meets the requirements described above will be acting lawfully.

Under the legislative amendments to the regulation of picketing in the LRA that are effective from 1 January 2015, the CCMA is able to establish rules allowing for picketing by employees in a place which is owned or controlled by a person other than the employer, provided that person has had an opportunity to make representations to the CCMA before the rules are established. This has the effect of permitting employees to picket on the private property of a third party who is not the employer, e.g., in a shopping mall belonging to a landlord in which the employer has a retail outlet.

As part of a legislative intervention strategy to try and curb protracted and violent strikes, amendments to the LRA introduced with effect from 1 January 2019 provide for an advisory arbitration panel to be established to try and resolve strikes or lockouts that are intractable, violent or which may cause a national crisis. The director of the CCMA may appoint such a panel where circumstances of public interest demand it or if directed to do so by the Minister of Labour. In certain circumstances, the parties to the industrial action or other interested parties may also apply for the establishment of the panel. The panel is required to investigate without delay the cause and circumstances of the industrial action and to make an advisory award aimed at assisting the parties in dispute to resolve the dispute. The appointment of the panel does not interrupt or suspend the industrial action. Once an advisory award has been issued, the parties have seven days in which to accept or reject the award and, where a party does not indicate its acceptance or rejection within this period, it will be deemed to have accepted the award which will then be binding on it.

The same amendments to the LRA also introduced:

- An obligation on trade unions to conduct a secret ballot of their affected members when seeking to call a strike (previously the ballot was not required secret). This is aimed at trying to ensure that strikes are only resorted to when the bulk of the affected members support the strike.
- Stricter regulation of picketing during industrial action, the thrust of which is to prohibit a picket unless there are picketing rules in place. Picketing rules can be put in place either by agreement between the parties or by the imposition by the CCMA where the parties cannot agree. The Labour Court is also given the power to suspend a picket if picketing rules are breached.

With effect from 19 December 2018, a Code of Good Practice: Collective Bargaining, Industrial Action and Picketing was also introduced, which provides practical guidance on collective bargaining, the resolution of disputes of mutual interest and the resort to industrial action (including picketing). The code includes template default picketing rules which are likely to be applied, adapted for the peculiarities of the industrial action in question if the CCMA is to impose picketing rules where the parties are unable to agree on such rules.

9.2. Right of Employees to Join Unions

All employees are permitted to form and join a trade union of their choice. Employees – through their trade unions – are also permitted to establish workplace forums in their workplace (although hardly any such forums have been established). It is prohibited to prejudice an employee for joining or participating in a trade union or to prevent him/her from doing so.

9.3. How Employees Select Unions

An employee may apply to be a member of any trade union. However, some unions only accept employees from certain industries.

A trade union may approach an employer for access to the workplace in order to recruit members. The employer is not obliged to agree to such access unless the union is sufficiently representative of the employees in the workplace. What will constitute 'sufficiently representative' will vary depending on each case but, as a general guideline, if the union has as its members approximately 25% of the employer's workforce when it requests access, it is likely to be entitled to access (although from 1 January 2015, the extent to which there are alternative workforce workers in the workplace is also taken into account which may mean that lower levels of representation may suffice – *see* below in this regard). Sufficient representation is also the test for a union to acquire the right to have the employer deduct union dues from its members pay and pay such dues over to the union, and for the right for an employee who is a union office bearer to be granted reasonable leave during working hours in order to perform the function of his/her office.

In order to secure a right to have the employees who are its members elect shop stewards (union representatives in the workplace), and a right to disclosure of information from the employer to allow shop stewards to effectively perform their functions, a trade union must show that it has the majority of the employees in the workplace as its members.

Where an employer refuses to grant a union the organizational rights referred above, the union can invoke a dispute resolution process presided over by the CCMA in which the union's level of representation and its rights are determined.

When the CCMA is determining whether organizational rights are to be awarded, it is required to seek to minimize both the proliferation of union representation in a single workplace and the administrative and financial burden of requiring the employer to grant organizational rights to more than one union. The CCMA must also consider factors such as the nature of the workplace, the organizational history at the workplace and the composition of the workforce taking into account the extent to which there are alternative workforce employees in the workplace (e.g., leased workers, fixed-term and part-time employees). Because alternative workforce workers have traditionally been harder to organize, lower levels of union representation in workplaces where such workers are present may be regarded as sufficient. Also, even where a collective agreement concluded with a majority union sets higher thresholds for basic organizational rights, a registered trade union which represents a 'significant amount' or a 'substantial number of employees' in the workplace may still be granted basic organizational rights.

9.4. Pre-election Campaigning

Trade unions and employers may try to lawfully persuade employees to either join or not join the trade union. Neither unions nor employers are permitted to intimidate employees either to join or not join the union. Employers may not promise or give an advantage (such as promotions or better wages) to an employee in exchange for the employee not joining a union, nor may the employer prejudice any employee because they elect to join a union.

The election process usually takes place at the employer's premises through a voting exercise with ballots. The employer usually observes but does not run the election process.

9.5. Unfair Labour Practices

The LRA defines certain specific forms of unfair conduct by an employer as constituting an unfair labour practice. This includes any unfair act or omission that arises between an employer and employee relating to promotions, demotions, probation, training, benefits, suspensions, refusals to reinstate an employee in terms of an agreement and occupational detriments against whistleblowers. For example, an employee who has been unfairly demoted can seek a determination from the CCMA that his demotion is an unfair labour practice. The CCMA can award reinstatement, re-employment or compensation (depending on what the CCMA determines is reasonable) against an employer who is found to have committed an unfair labour practice. Compensation can be up to twelve months' remuneration.

The LRA also prohibits behaviour that prejudices employees and job applicants because of their union activity. It provides that no person may discriminate against an employee for exercising any rights in relation to trade union membership and participation in its activities, and includes specific prohibitions of the following:

- requiring an employee or job applicant not to join a union or to give up union membership;
- prejudicing an employee or job applicant for union membership or participating in lawful union activities;
- promising advantage or advantaging an employee or job applicant in exchange for them not exercising a right relating to trade union membership.

If an employer dismisses an employee for a reason that contravenes these protections, the dismissal will be automatically unfair, and the employer may be held liable for up to two years' pay as compensation for the unfairness.

9.6. Relocation of Work/Shutdown of Business

Where an employer contemplates a closing or relocating of its business that may result in redundancies, the employer will generally be required to consult the trade unions with members in the business who will be affected. The consultation must take place in accordance with the applicable provisions of the LRA (section 189), and be completed before any decisions are made to close or relocate.

Where there is a statutory workplace forum in a particular workplace, then the employer is obliged to consult the workplace forum. (As indicated earlier, however, there are very few statutory workplace forums in existence in South Africa as such a body can only be established with the support of a trade union and most unions are against their establishment).

9.7. Checklist of Do's and Don'ts

- Do not ask job applicants questions about union membership in job interviews.
- Do not prejudice any employees or job applicants because of their union membership or activities.
- When unions claim organizational rights such as access to the workplace and stop orders, ask for proof of their representation before agreeing to grant them the rights sought, and verify the proof offered.
- You can try to persuade workers not to join a union, but do not promise them some form of advantage in exchange for not joining.
- Consult any unions who have members in the workplace before making any final decisions about closing or relocating business.

10. WORKING CONDITIONS: HOURS OF WORK AND PAYMENT OF WAGES – BY STATUTE OR COLLECTIVE AGREEMENTS

10.1. Overview of Wage and Hours Laws

The National Minimum Wage Bill (NMW Act) came into effect on 1 January 2019.

It will apply to all workers and employers in South Africa, except members of the South African Defence Force, the National Intelligence Agency and the South African Secret Service.

The NMW Act prescribes a national minimum wage of ZAR 20 per hour, with the exception of the farm/forestry sector, domestic worker sector and expanded public works programme sector, as they have been given a longer transition period. The minimum wage for these sectors is as follows:

- The minimum wage for farmworkers will be set at ZAR 18 per hour from 1 May 2018.
- The minimum wage for domestic workers will be set at ZAR 15 per hour from 1 May 2018.
- Workers employed on an expanded works public works programme are entitled to ZAR 11 per hour from 1 May 2018.

Employers or an employers' organization may apply for an exemption from paying the national minimum wage, for a period of no more than one year. This will only be considered if the delegated authority is satisfied that the employer or employers' organization could not afford to pay the minimum wage.

Minimum wages have been set for certain sectors and industries. This is done through either sectoral determinations issued by the Minister of Labour (e.g., farmworkers), or Bargaining Council Agreements (e.g., in the metal and engineering industries). The minimum wage will differ from sector to sector, and also varies by category of employees within the industry in question. Sometimes minimum wages differentiate between geographical areas, with a higher minimum for urban and a lower minimum for rural areas. Under powers granted to the Minister in terms of the BCEA, the Minister will in future be able to publish a sectoral determination to cover all employers and employees who are not covered by any other sectoral determination.

Certain minimum standards are set in the BCEA for hours of work and overtime. Sectoral determinations and bargaining council collective agreements for specific industries also regulate work hours. Generally, no employee may work more than forty-five ordinary hours a week and nine hours a day if he or she works a five-day week, or eight hours a day if he or she works a six-day week. Total working hours may not exceed twelve hours a day. Wage regulating measures specific to industries can have different provisions regulating working hours.

10.2. Minimum Wage

As indicated above, as from the beginning of 2019, there are no national minimum wages that apply to employees. In the sectors where minimum wages are set by sectoral determinations issued by the Minister of Labour, if the minimum wage is lower than the national minimum wage, the latter prevails. The main mechanism through which minimum wages are bargained and set is a negotiation at bargaining councils. Employer organizations and trade unions that are parties to these councils meet and negotiate minimum wages and, if the parties are representative enough in the industry in question, the agreements concluded are extended by ministerial proclamation to be binding on all employers and employees in the industry.

In the case of an application for a general work visa, a certificate must be obtained from the Department of Labour confirming that the foreign worker's salary and benefits are not inferior to the average salary and benefits of citizens or permanent residents occupying similar positions in the Republic, and confirming that the contract stipulating the conditions of employment and signed by both the employer and the applicant is in line with the labour standards in the Republic.

10.3. Overtime

All employees, except those listed in section 10.8 below, are subject to the following overtime rules:

- an employer can only require an employee to work overtime if the employee has agreed to do so, and if the employee's consent is obtained on commencement of employment or within three months thereof, the consent lapses after twelve months and must be secured again by the employer, where after the consent does not lapse again;
- an employer must pay an employee at least one and a half times the employee's wage for overtime worked, or grant the employee paid time off (e.g., ninety minutes off for every sixty minutes overtime worked);
- employees are not permitted to work more than ten hours of overtime a week (or three hours overtime on a day if they work a nine-hour day).

Work done on Sundays must be remunerated at double the normal rate for each hour worked by the employee, or at time and a half if the employee ordinarily works on a Sunday. Employers can avoid paying higher Sunday rates by agreeing with their employees that they will be given paid time off equivalent to the difference in the value of the pay received by the employee for the Sunday and the prescribed Sunday rates.

Employers cannot require employees to work on public holidays unless by agreement. Where employees work on a public holiday that falls on an ordinary working day, they must be paid double their ordinary rate. If the public holiday on which they work falls on a day when the employees do not normally work, they must be paid their ordinary daily wage plus the amount earned by the employees for work done on that day.

10.4. Meal and Rest Periods

Employees who work continuously for more than five hours are entitled to a meal break of at least one hour. During a meal break, employees can only be required to perform duties that cannot be left unattended and which cannot be performed by another employee. Employees must be paid for meal breaks in which they are required to work or be available for work, and for any portion of the meal break that is longer than seventy-five minutes unless the employee lives on the premises.

In terms of the BCEA, employees are generally entitled to a daily rest period of at least twelve consecutive hours and a weekly rest period of at least thirty-six consecutive hours which must include a Sunday, unless otherwise agreed. The weekly rest period can by agreement be reduced by up to eight hours in a week if it is extended equivalently in the following week, or it can be replaced with a rest period of sixty hours every fourteen days.

10.5. Deductions from Wages

Employers may not make any deductions from wages unless: (a) the deduction is required or permitted by law (e.g., income tax deductions), collective agreement, court order or arbitration award; or (b) the employee has agreed in writing to the deduction in respect of a debt specified in the agreement. Although the legal position is not settled in this regard, the restriction in (b) probably means that the authorization from the employee can only validly be given at the time when a debt arises, as opposed to a general authorization given (often in a contract of employment) in advance of any debt arising. If the deduction is to reimburse the employer for loss or damage caused by the employee, further requirements apply:

- the loss must have occurred in the course of the employee's employment and must have been the employee's fault;
- the employer must follow a fair procedure and give the employee a reasonable opportunity to show why the deductions should not be made;
- the total amount of the debt must not exceed the actual amount of the loss; and
- the total deductions from the employee's remuneration must not exceed one-quarter of the employee's cash remuneration.

Deductions for goods purchased by the employee from the employer are permitted but must specify the nature and quantity of the goods.

10.6. Prohibited Conduct by an Employer

An employer must not require or accept any payment by or on behalf of an employee or potential employee in respect of the employment of, or the allocation of work to, any employee. Further, an employer must not require an employee or potential employee to purchase goods, products or services from the employer or from any business or person nominated by the employer.

There is an exception to the above prohibition to the effect that the prohibition does not prevent an employment contract or collective agreement requiring employee participation in a scheme involving the purchase of specific goods, products or services, if (a) the purchase is not prohibited by any other statute, and (b) the employee receives a financial benefit from participating in the scheme and (c) the price of any goods or services provided through the scheme is fair and reasonable. Although this exception provides scope for the operation of compulsory benefit schemes, such as occupational retirement funds and medical aid schemes, employers are faced with what can be a complicated task of having to establish that the price of any goods or services provided through the schemes is fair and reasonable.

10.7. Garnishment

The NCA regulates what deductions may be made from an employee's remuneration to pay the employee's creditors. The NCA provides for consumer debt counselling and extensive powers for courts to make debt re-arrangement orders.

An employer who deducts from an employee's remuneration to pay a creditor of the employee must pay within the time period stipulated in the applicable agreement or court order.

10.8. Exemptions to Wage and Hour Laws

There are a number of exemptions from the BCEA's provisions regulating working time. The main categories of employees who do not enjoy the BCEA protections in relation to working time (e.g., enhanced pay for overtime) are:

- senior managerial employees;
- sales staff who travel to customers' premises and regulate their own working hours;

– employees who work for less than twenty-four hours a month;
– employees who earn more than a BCEA earnings threshold.

The BCEA allows the parties to agree on alternate provisions for working time. For instance, the employer and the employee can agree on a shorter work week but longer daily hours at ordinary wages, provided that daily working hours do not exceed twelve hours, and provided that this does not result in the employee working longer than forty-five ordinary hours or ten overtime hours in any week, or working more than five days a week.

A collective agreement (which can only be concluded with a trade union, and not with the employees directly) can provide that working hours will be averaged over a certain period not exceeding four months, such that highs and lows of overtime work during the period are averaged. The limit on the amount of overtime that can be worked under an averaging arrangement is an average of five hours per week, as opposed to the usual ten hours per week when no averaging arrangement is in place. The first two averaging agreements that are concluded lapse after twelve months, but they can thereafter become permanent. A collective agreement can also extend the amount of overtime to fifteen hours a week for up to two months in any one year.

10.9. Child Labour

Under the BCEA, it is an offence to require or permit a child to work if the child is under 15 years of age or under the minimum school-leaving age (currently, the South African Schools Act requires children to attend school until the last school day of the year in which they turn 15 years of age or the completion of grade 9, whichever is first). It is thus an offence to employ a child in the year in which he turns 15 unless he has finished grade 9.

In addition, it is an offence to require or permit a child to perform work or provide services that are inappropriate for a person of that age or that place at risk the child's well-being, education, physical or mental health, or spiritual, moral or social development.

However, the Minister of Labour may issue regulations to prohibit or place conditions on work by children who are at least 15 years of age and are no longer subject to compulsory schooling in terms of any law.

10.10. Record-Keeping Requirements

10.10.1. Information That Must Be Maintained

An employer should maintain records of the keys particulars of employment of its employees, including those described in section 2.2 above.

In practice, for most medium- and larger-sized employers, these particulars will be reflected in written employment contracts concluded with their employees.

Records of the time worked by the employee, leave taken, the remuneration paid, and taxes and levies deducted from remuneration should be maintained throughout an employee's employment.

10.10.2. Records That Must Be Retained

The Immigration Act imposes record-keeping obligations and sanctions for non-compliance on every employer of a foreign national, regardless of the business's size or the number of employees. Stricter compliance is required for any employer with more than five employees or who has been found guilty of a prior offence under the Immigration Act.

Employers are obliged to retain certain records for a period of two years after employment ceases, including: a certified copy of the passport of the foreigner reflecting his or her personal particulars; a copy of the relevant visa or permanent residence permit of that foreigner; proof of the capacity in which the foreigner is or was employed; and a copy of the foreigner's IRP5 form or certificate of earnings and job description.

An employer is required to keep the particulars referred to in section 10.10.1 above, together with records of the time worked by the employee, the remuneration actually paid and the date of birth of the employee if under 18 years of age, for a period of three years after the termination of employment.

10.10.3. Failure to Maintain Required Records

Where an employer fails to keep a record required by the BCEA that is relevant to an employee's BCEA claim, in proceedings concerning an alleged contravention by the employer of the BCEA the burden will be on the employer to prove that it complied with the BCEA.

Non-compliance with record-keeping obligations in relation to foreign workers also amounts to an offence under the Immigration Act.

10.11. Reductions in Compensation Caused by Economic Downturn

The reduction of an employee's compensation in order to meet the pressures of an economic downturn is generally only possible in South Africa by agreement with the employee. Prior to the 2015 amendments to the LRA, it was clear that if due to an economic downturn an employer has to reduce compensation, it may consult with its employees (and their trade unions if applicable), and propose that employees accept a reduction as an alternative to their retrenchment. If by the end of the consultation process the employees do not accept the reduction in compensation required to meet the business' operational needs, the employer may retrench the employees and employ new employees who are prepared to work for the lower level of compensation. However, the amendments to the LRA effective from 1 January 2015 provide that a dismissal will be automatically unfair if the reason for the dismissal is 'a refusal by employees to accept a demand in respect of any matter of mutual interest between them and their employer'. This may limit the scope for an employer to dismiss employees for operational reasons where they have refused to accept an employer's demand relating to a change to their terms and conditions of employment that is operationally needed, but whether it goes this far and what its exact reach is remains to be seen.

10.12. Checklist of Do's and Don'ts

- Ensure that you pay the applicable national minimum wage.
- Before concluding contracts of employment, check if the industry in which you operate has a bargaining council or sectoral determination applicable to it which regulates working time and wages and make sure your proposed employment contract complies with the regulations and takes advantage of any dispensations catered for under the regulating measure (e.g., where the employer may contract out of normal working hours).
- Check whether the position in question is exempt from the working time protections.
- If the BCEA overtime regime applies to your employment contracts, renegotiate the obligation to work overtime after the first twelve months of an employee's employ.
- Do not deduct from remuneration unless the employee has agreed in writing to the deduction for the debt in question, or you have a court order or arbitration award authorizing the deduction.

- Consider whether any of the aspects of working time regulation from which you can depart by agreement would better suit your requirements and agree on the variations in writing with your employees/trade unions.
- Do not employ children under 15 years of age, and if they are 15, check if they have finished grade 9 before employing them.
- Consider whether the price of any goods or services provided to employees through compulsory benefit schemes is fair and reasonable.

11. OTHER WORKING CONDITIONS AND BENEFITS: BY STATUTE, COLLECTIVE AGREEMENTS OR COMPANY POLICY

11.1. Health and Other Insurance

There is currently no general obligation on employers in South Africa to provide health insurance to their employees. Many employers voluntarily participate in medical plans to secure medical benefits for their employees. Group life insurance benefits are also commonly provided by employers, yielding death benefits that are commonly equivalent to three times the employee's annual salary.

In industries that are regulated by bargaining councils, collective agreements concluded in the council will usually provide for compulsory contributions by both employers and employees to industry medical plans designed to provide basic medical benefits.

Unemployment is regulated by the UIA and the Unemployment Insurance Contributions Act. Both the employer and the employee must make monthly contributions to the unemployment insurance fund, which provides unemployment benefits to individuals who are temporarily unemployed. The employer should pay the total contribution of 2% to the Unemployment Insurance Fund. This total contribution is capped at remuneration not exceeding an amount stipulated by the Minister of Finance, which as of 2019 is ZAR 14,872 per month. The fund also provides limited maternity leave benefits for a maximum period of four months (the amounts payable depend on the employee's remuneration, and there are maximum thresholds, but generally lower earners can expect to get in the region of 30%–50% of their normal pay as a benefit).

11.2. Pension and Retirement Benefits

There is similarly no general obligation on employers in South Africa to provide pension or retirement benefits to their employees. However, it is anticipated that in the next few years, a compulsory national retirement saving scheme will be introduced that will entail obligatory contributions from employers and employees as savings for the employees' retirement. The exact nature and terms of the scheme are not yet determined.

Although there is no obligation to provide pension or retirement benefits, they are commonly provided by employers through a private pension or provident funds. Most retirement funds in the private sector are defined contribution funds where the employee members bear the investment risk in relation to the investment performance of their share of the fund.

In industries regulated by bargaining councils, collective agreements concluded in the council will usually provide for compulsory contributions by both employers and employees to industry retirement funds designed to provide basic retirement benefits and often funeral insurance.

11.3. Vacation and Holiday Payments on Termination

Under the BCEA, employees who work twenty-four hours or more per month are entitled to a minimum of twenty-one consecutive days (i.e., three weeks) paid leave per annual leave cycle of twelve months. Pay for annual leave must be based on the employee's normal remuneration. An employee is not entitled to take annual leave until he or she has completed the leave cycle in question, but most employers allow employees to take leave before the end of the cycle.

In some industries (e.g., construction) there is an annual shutdown period from mid-December to mid-January, during which employees are required to take their annual leave.

An employer and employee can agree that the employee's annual leave will accrue incrementally, which is often appropriate in cases where the employee works part-time or irregularly. The agreement in this regard can be either that the annual leave accrues at a rate of one day of leave for every seventeen days on which he or she worked or was entitled to be paid, or that it accrues at a rate of one hour of leave for every seventeen hours for which the employee worked or was entitled to be paid.

The timing of when annual leave is taken is subject to agreement between the parties, failing which it is the employer's prerogative to direct when leave must be taken.

When an employee departs employment, the employer is required to pay the employee for his or her annual leave that has accrued but has not been taken. Exactly how much leave can be accumulated and paid out on termination is currently legally uncertain in South Africa as there are conflicting Labour Court judgments on the issue. One judgment (*Jardine v. Tongaat-Hulett Sugar Ltd* [2003] 7 BLLR 717 (LC)) found that the BCEA does not set a ceiling on the amount of leave that may be accumulated beyond which leave is forfeited, while the other (*Jooste v. Kohler Packaging Ltd* [2003] 12 BLLR 1251 (LC)) held that, with respect to statutory annual leave, the only leave pay that was payable was for leave accrued in the leave cycle (a twelve-month period) immediately preceding that during which termination takes place as well as the pro rata entitlement for the current cycle. The approach in *Jooste* has been followed in a subsequent Labour Court case,[11] but the issue has yet to reach the more authoritative LAC, and until it does, the law in this area will remain uncertain.

11.4. Leaves of Absence

The BCEA's minimum benefits provisions in relation to leave apply to all employees with the exception only of employees who work for less than twenty-four hours a month.

11.4.1. Personal Leave

Leave for personal reason forms part of statutory family responsibility leave under South African law. *See* section 11.4.3 below. There is no statutory entitlement beyond that. Employers may have policies that grant such leave to employees, but there is no norm in this regard.

11.4.2. Medical or Sick Leave

For each sick leave cycle of thirty-six months of employment, an employee is entitled to paid sick leave equal to the number of days he or she would normally work during a period of six weeks. Thus, the sick leave entitlement of an employee working a five-day week is thirty days per thirty-six-month sick leave cycle.

During the first six months of employment, an employee is only entitled to one day of paid sick leave for every twenty-six days worked. Thereafter, the full sick leave entitlement is available to the employee at any stage during the sick leave cycle.

Under the BCEA, an employee is not entitled to payment for sick leave if he or she is absent from work for more than two consecutive days, or on more than two occasions during an eight-week period, unless he or she produces a medical certificate at the employer's request. This regime only

11. *Ludick v. Rural Maintenance (Pty.) Ltd*, unreported Case No. JS633/07, dated 30 Oct. 2013, per Van Niekerk J.

regulates when an employer does not have to pay for an absence due to sickness, and it does not prevent an employer from having a workplace rule that requires employees to produce a medical certificate for any day on which they are absent from work due to illness (or, e.g., for sick absences that occur immediately before or after weekends or public holidays). A breach of such a rule may not disqualify the employee from payment for the day's absence (by virtue of the BCEA) but would be considered an act of misconduct, which can assist in the employer's management of absenteeism.

11.4.3. Bereavement Leave

Leave for bereavement forms part of statutory family responsibility leave under South African law. Under the BCEA, employees are entitled to family responsibility leave of three days per annual leave cycle, which must be granted upon request of an employee when the employee's child is born or is sick, or upon the death of the employee's spouse or life partner or a parent, adoptive parent, grandparent, child, adopted child, grandchild or sibling.

Family responsibility leave lapses if not taken during an annual leave cycle.

11.4.4. Family Leave

Family leave is part of the BCEA's family responsibility entitlement.

11.4.5. Pregnancy Leave

Statutory leave for pregnancy forms part of the BCEA maternity leave. An employee is entitled to commence statutory maternity leave any time from four weeks before the expected date of birth (unless otherwise agreed) or on another date stipulated by a medical practitioner or midwife in the interest of the employee's health or that of her unborn child.

11.4.6. Maternity Leave

Under the BCEA, female employees are entitled to a minimum of four consecutive months of unpaid maternity leave. Although the BCEA does not require maternity leave to be paid by employers, many employers provide partial payment as a contractual benefit to their employees. Otherwise, some payment for maternity leave can be obtained by an employee under the limited social security legislation that exists in South Africa, particularly under the UIA. The amount of the benefit paid is limited and is generally well below the employee's usual level of remuneration.

The employee is not permitted to work for at least six weeks after giving birth unless she is declared fit to do so by a medical practitioner or midwife. An employee who has a miscarriage during her third trimester of pregnancy or bears a stillborn child is entitled to six weeks' maternity leave after the miscarriage or stillbirth, irrespective of whether she had already commenced maternity leave. An employee must give at least four weeks' written notice of the date when her intended maternity leave will commence, and when she will return to work or if giving four weeks' notice is not reasonably practicable, then notice must be given as soon as it is reasonably practicable to do so.

11.4.7. Parental, Adoption and Surrogacy Leave

Currently, the BCEA provides for three days family responsibility leave which can be taken by the father of a child when the child is born (and in other circumstances as discussed above). Therefore, at present, there are no paternal, adoptive or surrogacy leave benefits provided for in the BCEA (although an employee is entitled to claim adoption benefits from the Unemployment Insurance Fund (UIF), which is generally only payable if the employee is on unpaid leave for a period of time after adoption.

In late 2019, the Labour Laws Amendment Act was passed, but it is not yet operative. It will amend both the BCEA and the UIA by including provisions for parental, adoption and commissioning parental leave, as well as the payment of parental and commissioning parental benefits from the UIF.

The proposed amendments in this regard are as follows:

- An employee who is a parent is entitled to ten consecutive days' parental leave when that employee's child is born or when an adoption order is granted.
- An employee who is an adoptive parent of a child who is younger than two years is entitled to adoption leave of ten weeks consecutively. Note that if there are two adoptive parents, only one of the employees is entitled to adoption leave, and the other employee is entitled to parental leave. The selection or choice must be exercised at the option of the two parents.
- An employee who is a prospective adoptive parent of a child who is younger than two years is entitled to adoption leave of ten weeks consecutively from the date that the child is placed with the prospective adoptive parent in terms of a court order. As with adoptive parents, if there

are two prospective adoptive parents, one of the employees is entitled to adoption leave, and the other employee is entitled to parental leave.

– An employee who is a commissioning parent in a surrogate motherhood agreement is entitled to commissioning parental leave of ten weeks consecutively. As with adoption leave, if there are two commissioning parents, one of the employees is entitled to commissioning parental leave, and the other employee is entitled to parental leave.

The amendments are gender-neutral and allow for surrogacy and adoption of parental benefits.

11.4.8. Injury at Work

Employers are obliged to pay compensation to employees temporarily disabled by an injury at work for the first three months of their absence from work. The rate of compensation payable is determined by COIDA. The compensation paid by the employer is repaid to it after the first three months by the Compensation Fund established under COIDA. After the first three months, then compensation may be payable to the employee by the Compensation Fund in the form of periodical payments as determined by COIDA.

COIDA operates on a 'no-fault' basis in that employees who are injured at work or who contract occupational diseases are entitled to compensation regardless of whether the accident was caused by their employer or any other employee. However, compensation for injuries is based on the degree of disablement and employees may be entitled to increased compensation if their disablement is caused by the carelessness of their employer or a fellow employee. Claims for compensation are submitted to the Compensation Fund for consideration. Employers make regular contributions to this fund, and in return, employees are prevented from instituting damages claims against their employers in respect of an occupational injury or disease.

This approach has advantages for both employers and employees. On the one hand, employers are not subjected to costly damages claims, and on the other hand, employees are able to receive compensation without having to prove that another person's negligence caused the occupational injury or disease.

All employers, with certain limited exceptions, such as national or provincial governments, municipalities and employees permitted to obtain separate insurance policies in respect of their potential liability, must register with the Compensation Fund and contribute to it. The responsibility for the administration of the fund rests with the Department of Labour which in turn has delegated this responsibility to the Compensation Commissioner.

An employee is entitled to compensation in the event that the employee suffers a temporary or permanent disability. In the event of the death of an employee as a result of an occupational injury or disease, the dependants of the deceased employee are entitled to compensation. The extent of compensation due to an employee or a dependant is determined with reference to a schedule in COIDA, which also prescribes minimum and maximum compensation due in different circumstances.

11.5. Checklist of Do's and Don'ts

- Because there are no general regulated medical and retirement benefits, if you are going to provide such benefits to your employees, take advantage of the fact that you can choose arrangements that best suit your objectives as the employer.
- Reserve a right to change medical or retirement plans.
- The regulation of leave described above applies only to minimum statutory leave under the BCEA – if employers grant leave benefits in excess thereof they are free to make arrangements relating to the extra benefits without having regard to the BCEA regulations.
- All employers must register with the Compensation Fund and make regular contributions in respect of their employees.
- All claims must be timely submitted to the Compensation Fund.
- The employer must co-operate with the Compensation Fund and the employee to ensure that the necessary claim forms are completed.

12. WORKER'S COMPENSATION

Workman's compensation is dealt with in the COIDA, 1993. *See* section 11.4.8 above and the checklist that follows under section 11.5.

13. COMPANY'S OBLIGATION TO PROVIDE SAFE AND HEALTHY WORKPLACE

13.1. Overview of Safety and Environmental Laws and Regulations

Health and safety in the workplace are primarily regulated by OHSA. However, certain industries, such as mining, have specialized health and safety legislation.

All employees have a common law right to a safe working environment. OHSA supplements this right and protects employees and all persons present at a workplace. Further, the obligations imposed under OHSA apply to the employer's own premises and any other place where the employees are required to perform their functions. Therefore, should the employees of an employer operate at different premises, the employer is obliged to ensure that each premises complies with the requirements of OHSA.

13.2. Requirements

Under OHSA, employers are required to:

- act in a manner which is conducive to health and safety;
- report incidents to a health and safety inspector;
- ensure that a system of safety committees and representatives is introduced and operates at their establishment;
- ensure, as far as reasonably practicable, a safe and healthy working environment;
- not expose a worker to working conditions that are unsafe;
- provide and maintain systems of work, plant and machinery that are safe and without risk to the health of employees;
- take steps to eliminate or mitigate any risk to the health or safety of employees, before resorting to the use of personal protective equipment;
- ensure that the production, processing, use, handling, storage or transport of articles or substances are safe and free from risk to health and safety;
- conduct investigations to determine whether there are any hazards to the health or safety of employees, and establish precautionary measures to minimize the identified hazards;
- provide employees with information, instructions, training and supervision to enable them to protect themselves at work;
- not permit employees to do any work unless the necessary precautionary measures have been taken;
- ensure that all employees and other persons on the employer's premises comply with the provisions of OHSA;
- ensure that work is performed under the supervision of an individual trained in safety issues and able to take precautionary measures.

Employers also have a general duty to persons other than their employees to take steps to ensure that their business is conducted in such a manner that it does not pose a risk to the health and safety of all these persons at the employers' premises.

13.3. Rights of Employees

An employee has the right to work in a safe and healthy environment and to report any incidents which affect this right without victimization. Where an employee cannot perform his duties without a risk to health and safety, then such an employee is entitled to be supplied with the necessary personal protective equipment and would be entitled to refuse to perform work when it is unsafe to do so. Employees are also entitled to any information, instructions, training and supervision to enable them to protect themselves at work.

13.4. Rights of Employer

Other than the obvious right to defend itself at an enquiry into an accident or fatality at the workplace, OHSA does not grant employers any rights as such. This is because the focus of OHSA is on placing obligations on employers to ensure compliance with health and safety standards. Employers are entitled to dismiss employees for misconduct in serious cases where employees refuse to comply with OHSA. In general, employees are required to:

- take reasonable care for their own health and safety, and the health and safety of other employees;
- co-operate with the employer or any other designated person in relation to health and safety matters;
- report any unsafe or unhealthy situation to the employer or a health and safety representative;
- refrain from interfering with, or misusing anything provided for health and safety;
- employees are required to carry out any lawful order given to them and obey the health and safety rules and procedures laid down by his employer or by anyone authorized by his employer, in the interest of health or safety;
- report any incident which the employee is involved in and which may affect his health or which has caused him to sustain an injury, to his employer or to anyone authorized thereto by the employer, or to his health and safety representative, as soon as practicable. The employee must report the incident by no later than the end of the particular shift during which the incident occurred unless the circumstances were such that the reporting of the incident was not possible, in which case he shall report the incident as soon as practicable thereafter.

13.5. Specific Standards

The Minister of Labour may make specific regulations which are considered necessary or expedient in the interest of health and safety at the workplace. The Minister may further incorporate any health and safety standard into the regulations. Extensive regulations relating to general safety, machinery, electrical and environmental pressure vessels, etc., have been made. These regulations are amended from time to time, and it is important that employers keep abreast of the passing of any new regulations as well as the amendment of any regulations in order to remain compliant.

13.6. Injury or Accident at Work

An employer must report incidents which result in the death, illness or injury of an employee to a health and safety inspector. The employer is also required to investigate incidents and to record the findings. The record of the investigation must also be made available to a health and safety committee if there is one in the workplace. The duty to report incidents is in addition to the reporting requirements imposed on employers by COIDA to report any workplace accident to the Compensation Commissioner.

In the decision of the Supreme Court of Appeal in *MEC for the Department of Health, Free State Province v. D* (924/2013) [2014] ZASCA 167; 2015 (1) SA 182 (SCA); [2015] 1 All SA 20 (SCA); [2014] 12 BLLR 1155 (SCA); (2014) 35 ILJ 3301 (SCA) (8 October 2014), the court accepted that an employee may still have a claim in delict against an employer for illness or injuries sustained in the workplace if such injury or illness does not arise out of and in the course and scope of employment. However, a sufficient causal connection between the accident and the employee's employment or work must exist before the provisions of COIDA may apply.

13.7. Workplace Violence

There are no specific provisions in OHSA which deal with workplace violence. Injuries suffered as a consequence of workplace violence can be dealt with in terms of OHSA in terms of the general duty of employers to provide and maintain a working environment that is safe and without risk to the health of employees and any negligence arising therefrom.

13.8. Fines and Penalties

The Chief Executive Officer (CEO) of a company is held liable for the company's compliance with OHSA and its regulations. It is, therefore, the CEO who will be cited in legal proceedings and who will be subject to the penalties imposed below. This applies even where there has been a delegation of the CEO's responsibilities to another person.

Any person who contravenes OHSA can be fined a maximum of ZAR 50,000 or be imprisoned for a maximum of one year, or both. Where the contravention results in injury or death, the maximum fine and period of imprisonment is increased to ZAR 100,000 or two years respectively, or both.

13.9. Checklist of Do's and Don'ts

- Conduct ongoing, documented workplace evaluations to identify all hazards to employee health and safety. This evaluation should include input from all employees who may be affected by such hazards.
- Conduct documented training to ensure compliance with health and safety requirements.
- Conduct regular health and safety audits to ensure compliance with health and safety requirements.
- Ensure that outside contractors are familiar with the health and safety rules applicable to the company and that they have informed their own staff about these rules.

14. IMMIGRATION, SECONDMENT AND FOREIGN ASSIGNMENT

14.1. Overview Laws Controlling Immigration

The Immigration Act No. 13 of 2002 as amended, read with Immigration Regulations 2014, as implemented on 26 May 2014, regulates the admission of persons to, their residence in, and their departure from South Africa, and the employment of foreign nationals in South Africa. In particular, it provides for the issuance of different categories of temporary visas and permanent residence permits, including work visas.

The Department of Home Affairs also issues various practice directives which influence the execution and application of the law.

Any foreigner who is not a permanent resident, a refugee or a political asylum seeker and who wishes to render services in South Africa needs to obtain an appropriate authorization to work under the Immigration Act. A separate residence visa is not required because a temporary residence work visa confers the right to both work and reside in South Africa. As soon as the intended activities of the foreigner meet the definition of work, an appropriate authorization to work is required, irrespective of the duration for which services will be rendered in South Africa.

The Immigration Act provides that it is a criminal offence to employ a foreign national who does not hold a work permit or to employ them in a position or capacity other than what is authorized in their work permit. Sanctions for non-compliance with the duties and obligations placed on the employer of a foreign national apply to all employers, regardless of size or number of employees, although stricter compliance is required of an employer who employs more than five employees or has been found guilty of a prior offence under the Act.

14.2. Recruiting, Screening and Hiring Process

The recruitment, screening and hiring process to be followed will depend on the category of work visa being applied for. All offers of employment must be made subject to the employee obtaining and maintaining the appropriate work visa at all relevant times during the employment.

A certificate is required from the Department of Labour confirming that despite a diligent search, the prospective employer has been unable to find a suitable citizen or permanent resident with qualifications or skills and experience equivalent to those of the applicant and that the salary and benefits of the applicant are not inferior to the average salary and benefits of citizens or permanent residents occupying similar positions in the Republic, and confirming that the contract stipulating the conditions of employment and signed by both the employer and the applicant is in line with the labour standards in the Republic and is made conditional upon the general work visa being approved.

Although it is no longer mandatory to advertise the position in terms of regulation, the Department of Labour still requires such advertisement in order to certify compliance with labour-market-testing obligations. Additionally, all opportunities must be registered on the Department of Labour's ESSA registration database. The Department of Labour also requires a report from a professional recruitment agency and in certain industries or locations, from tribal leaders, on the availability of South Africans to fill the position. It must be demonstrated that it is justifiable or necessary to appoint a foreign worker to the position. Where applications are received from locals, the employer is obliged to interview applicants who appear to be suitable and to provide reasons for the unsuitability of any

South African applicants. Interview notes must be submitted to the Department of Labour in order to procure their certification in support of the application.

Applicants who apply for spousal or life partner work permits on the basis of their relationship with a South African citizen or permanent resident need not comply with this requirement.

Posts may also be offered to applicants for critical skills work visas and intra-company transfer work visas without the need for labour-market testing.

The recruitment process for hiring foreign employees, as set out above, must take place *before* the worker can apply for the relevant visa, unless a waiver of the requirement to submit certification from the Department of Labour is obtained, which may be obtained by way of a separate waiver application to the Department of Home Affairs, preceding the work visa application.

Where an existing foreign employee's work authorization expires, the employer must ensure that such employee is in possession of a new or renewed permit before the expiry date of the initial permit, failing which employment may not continue until the new permit is obtained, as a pending application does not afford the applicant status in South Africa.

14.3. The Obligation of Employer to Enforce Immigration Laws

Companies are obliged to confirm that foreign employees hold the appropriate visa to work for a particular company in the specified position before commencing employment.

The Immigration Act provides that no assistance may be provided to an illegal foreigner, save for the necessary humanitarian assistance and that anyone aiding and abetting an illegal foreigner is guilty of a criminal offence.

The employment of illegal foreigners, a foreigner whose status does not authorize them to be employed, as well as the employment of foreigners on terms and conditions or in a capacity different from those contemplated by such foreigner's status, is prohibited.

The provisions of the Immigration Act give rise to a legal presumption that where an illegal foreigner is found on any premises where the business is conducted, such foreigner was employed by the person who has control over such premises unless evidence to the contrary is produced.

It is no defence to claim that the status of the foreigner was unknown to the employer if such employer ought reasonably to have known the status of the foreigner, based on the prevailing circumstances.

Employers of foreign nationals are obliged to ensure that the foreigner maintains valid status and to notify the Department of Home Affairs of any change of conditions to the foreigner's employment, and of any contravention by the foreigner of his status, which becomes known to the employer.

Employers are also obliged to maintain certain records for a period of two years after employment ceases.

14.4. Fines and Penalties

Employing foreigners without an appropriate work visa can result in severe sanctions, with the company facing fines and, possible imprisonment of company officials, and the illegal worker potentially facing detention and deportation.

The Department of Home Affairs seeks enforcement of maximum penalties where there is a pattern or practice of knowingly hiring illegal foreigners.

The Immigration Act and the regulations thereto provide that anyone who has previously been deported and has since not been rehabilitated by the Director General, an automatically prohibited person, thereby disqualifying them from obtaining a port of entry visa, admission into the Republic, a visa or permanent residence. Anyone found in possession of a fraudulent permanent residence permit, port of entry visa, passport or identification document is also automatically rendered a prohibited person.

Similarly, foreigners may be declared undesirable by the Director General if they have been ordered to depart in terms of the Immigration Act or have overstayed their visa. After such declaration, they will not qualify for a port of entry visa, admission into the Republic, a visa or permanent residence.

14.5. Secondment/Foreign Assignment

South African employment laws generally do not apply to South African nationals working abroad. They may, however, apply to a South African national who works abroad temporarily on secondment, especially if the employment contract provides for South African law to apply.

Although it is not legally mandatory, it is common to formalize employment contracts that involve a foreign assignment in writing. Even if no written employment contract is concluded, an employer must supply any employee certain prescribed information in writing at the commencement of their service. Visa applications require the submission of written contracts signed by both employee and employer. Certain visa categories, such as general work visas, require the conclusion of a local contract. The Department of Home Affairs generally insists on the foreign employment not terminating for the duration of placement in South Africa on an intra-company transfer visa.

South African employment laws are mandatory for any employees that fall within their jurisdiction. They, therefore, apply to foreign nationals working in South Africa. A Labour Court decision has held that this is the case, even if the foreign nationals are working here illegally.

A foreign employer who deploys its employees to work in South Africa will be taken to be a party to a contract of employment within South Africa, as a consequence of which it will be obliged to register with the South African Companies and Intellectual Property Commission as an external company under section 23 of the South African Companies Act, 2008. Such employers also need to be aware that their pursuit of business in South Africa may result in them being regarded as having a permanent establishment for tax purposes in South Africa.

14.6. Checklist of Do's and Don'ts

- Create a reporting and documentation control process for all foreign employees and their family members which ensures that document checking and record-keeping procedures are aligned with regulation.
- Develop internal policy guidelines and protocols, setting out the processes to be followed by HR and expatriates for each of the different work visa categories.
- Establish effective lines of communication between business units, especially HR/Legal division/line management of foreign workers.
- Ensure HR Managers are trained to determine, enforce and monitor legislative and regulatory compliance and, in particular, that the expiry dates of permits visas are monitored.
- Ensure accurate and timely information transfer to external professional support and ensure that all facts are relayed as fully and timeously as possible, as even seemingly unimportant information can have dire consequences.

15. RESTRICTIVE COVENANTS AND PROTECTION OF TRADE SECRETS AND CONFIDENTIAL INFORMATION

15.1. Overview

Restraint of trade (i.e., non-compete) protections are often included in employment contracts, but usually for more senior employees who are privy to the employer's most confidential information or critical customer relationships. Such provisions are in principle valid, and many restraints are enforced in South African courts every year. However, the courts will not enforce them if, in a particular case, such enforcement would be contrary to the public interest or unreasonable.

Disclosure of an employer's trade secrets and confidential information is prohibited under the common law, but most employers include specific non-disclosure provisions in their written contracts of employment.

15.2. The Law of Trade Secrets

Generally speaking, information will be a trade secret or confidential information warranting protection if it is information relating to the employer's business which has economic value and which is not available to its competitors or in the public domain. At common law, employees may not use their employer's trade secrets or confidential information for their own benefit or the benefit of a third party without their employer's consent. If the employer suffers damages as a result of a breach of this obligation, the employee can be held liable for the damages. Breach of a contractual obligation to protect trade secrets and confidential information may also give rise to a claim for damages. Damages are often hard to prove, and in many instances, the more effective legal remedy is to obtain an injunction to prevent the threatened or continued misuse of the information.

15.3. Restrictive Covenants and Non-compete Agreements

Like any contract in South Africa, a restraint of trade (non-compete) obligation will generally not be enforceable if its enforcement would be contrary to the public interest. In the case of restraints, if it is unreasonable, its enforcement will generally not be in the public interest. The reasonableness of the restraint is typically judged on two factors: the broad interests of the public and the interests of the contracting parties themselves. The broad interests of the public require the courts to balance two conflicting concerns: that agreements solemnly entered into should be upheld and enforced; and that persons should generally be free to engage in economic activity, and should not be rendered unproductive.

Reasonableness depends on many factors, the most important of which are:

- Whether the employer has a protectable interest that may legitimately be protected by means of a restraint agreement. Protectable interests include trade secrets and other confidential information; know-how; customer lists and connections; and goodwill. Interests that are not protectable include a business's interest in eliminating the competition and investment of time and money in training an employee.
- Whether the protectable interest is being infringed by the employee's conduct and if so whether the protectable interest is sufficiently weighty (qualitatively and quantitatively) when measured against the employee's interest in being economically active, that it should be protected by the enforcement of the restraint.
- Whether there is any other facet of public policy having nothing to do with the employment relationship that requires the enforcement or rejection of the restraint.
- The geographical area of the restraint.
- The duration of the restraint.
- Whether any (financial) consideration has been given for the restraint (although this is not a prerequisite to the enforcement of the restraint).

Less important, but not entirely irrelevant, is whether there was a concession by the employee that the restraint is reasonable, and equality of bargaining power when it was concluded.

The restraint should go no further than is necessary to protect the proprietary interests of the employer. Where it goes too far, the court may, in some instances, order partial enforcement (e.g., for a lesser period or within a more circumscribed territory) or it may decline to enforce it at all.

The restraint may also be combined in appropriate cases with a period of paid gardening leave during a notice period. In such cases, the reasonable period of the restraint and the period of gardening leave must be viewed cumulatively (*see Vodacom (Pty) Ltd v. Motsa and Another* 2016 (3) SA 116 (LC)).

15.4. Checklist of Do's and Don'ts

- Include express obligations in contracts of employment prohibiting the misuse of confidential information and trade secrets.

- Include restraint of trade obligations in the contracts of those employees who have access to confidential information or who hold customer relationships.
- Make sure that the scope of the restraint obligations is reasonable under the circumstances (this may differ from employee to employee). The geographic scope should be limited to the area in which the employee could unfairly exploit your confidential information or customer connections and the period of the restraint should be limited to a period that is long enough to result in the confidential information becoming stale or to enable you to re-establish the customer connections (periods between approximately six and twenty-four months have been enforced in appropriate cases).

16. PROTECTION OF WHISTLEBLOWING CLAIMS

16.1. Overview

The Protected Disclosures Act No. 26 of 2000 (PDA) has been amended by The Protected Disclosures Amendment Act No. 5 of 2017 (PDAA).The amendments have been made, so as to extend the application and protection afforded by the PDA, to include not only employees but workers as well, i.e., individuals currently or previously employed by the state as well as independent contractors, consultants, agents and those rendering services to a client while being employed by a 'temporary employment service' (i.e., a labour broker).

The Act is designed to facilitate the disclosure of information by employees or workers relating to criminal and other irregular conduct in the workplace in a responsible manner by providing comprehensive statutory guidelines for the disclosure of such information and to provide for immunity against civil and criminal liability flowing from a disclosure of information which shows or tends to show that a criminal offence has been committed, is being committed or is reasonably likely to be committed; to create an offence for the disclosure of false information; and to provide for matters connected therewith.

A 'disclosure' means any disclosure of information regarding any conduct of an employer, or of an employee or of a worker of that employer, made by any employee or worker who has a reason to believe that the information concerned shows or tends to show one or more of the following:

(a) that a criminal offence has been committed, is being committed or is likely to be committed;
(b) that a person has failed, is failing or is likely to fail to comply with any legal obligation to which that person is subject;

(c) that a miscarriage of justice has occurred, is occurring or is likely to occur;
(d) that the health or safety of an individual has been, is being or is likely to be endangered;
(e) that the environment has been, is being or is likely to be damaged;
(f) unfair discrimination as contemplated in Chapter II of the EEA No. 55 of 1998, or the Promotion of Equality and Prevention of Unfair Discrimination Act (PEPUDA) No. 4 of 2000; or
(g) that any matter referred to in paragraphs (a)–(f) has been, is being or is likely to be deliberately concealed.

An employee or worker who has made a protected disclosure may not be subjected to any 'occupational detriment'. This includes disciplinary action, dismissal, suspension, demotion, harassment or intimidation; being transferred against his or her will; being refused transfer or promotion; being subjected to a term or condition of employment or retirement which is altered or kept altered to his or her disadvantage; being refused a reference, or being provided with an adverse reference; being denied appointment to any employment, profession or office; being threatened with any of the actions previously referred to; or being otherwise adversely affected in respect of his or her employment, profession or office, including employment opportunities and work security.

The definition of 'occupational detriment' has also been extended to include being subjected to a civil claim for the alleged breach of a duty of confidentiality or a confidentiality agreement arising out of the disclosure of a criminal offence or information which shows or tends to show that a substantial contravention or failure to comply with the law has occurred, is occurring or is likely to occur.

Disclosure to an employer will be protected under the PDA if it was made in good faith and substantially in accordance with any procedure prescribed or authorized by the employer for reporting or otherwise remedying the impropriety concerned.

There is now also an obligation on employers to authorize appropriate internal procedures for receiving and dealing with information about improprieties and take reasonable steps to bring the internal procedures to the attention of every employee and worker.

The PDA amendments introduced a new provision in terms of which an employee or worker who intentionally discloses false information knowing that the information is false with the intention to cause harm to the affected party and the affected party suffered harm as a result of such disclosure is guilty of an offence. This conduct would constitute an offence even if an employee or worker 'ought reasonably to have known' that the information being disclosed is false. If an employee or worker is found guilty of this offence, he or she would be liable on conviction to a fine or to imprisonment for a period not exceeding two years or to both such fine and such imprisonment.

An employee or worker can also claim protection for disclosures to a third party where he genuinely believes that, if he makes the disclosure to his employer, he will be subjected to an occupational detriment, or he has reason to believe that it is likely that evidence relating to the impropriety will be concealed or destroyed if he makes the disclosure to his employer, or he has previously made a disclosure of substantially the same information to the employer (or body designated by the employer), or the impropriety is of an exceptionally serious nature. He must also reasonably believe that the information disclosed is substantially true, it must be generally reasonable to have made the disclosure, and he must not make it for any personal gain (other than a reward payable by law).

The amended PDA also provides for joint liability where an employer and its client are jointly and severally liable for those instances where the employer 'under the express or implied authority or with the knowledge of a client' subjects an employee or worker to an occupational detriment.

A further provision introduced in the amended PDA is the duty to inform an employee or worker of the steps taken once a disclosure has been made. In this respect, employers are required to, as soon as reasonably possible, but within a period of twenty-one days after receiving the protected disclosure, decide whether to investigate the matter or refer the disclosure to another person or body. The employer is also required to acknowledge receipt of the disclosure in writing by informing the employee or worker of its decision to investigate the matter or to refer it to another person or body. Should an employer be unable to make a decision within this time period, the employer will be required to inform the employee or worker, in writing, that it is unable to do so and, thereafter, advise the employee or worker on a regular basis (at intervals of not more than two months at a time) that the decision is still pending. In such instance, the employer is required to advise the employee or worker of its decision on whether to investigate the matter as soon as reasonably possible but within a period of six months after the protected disclosure has been made.

An employer need not comply with the duty to advise an employee or worker of its decision on whether or not to investigate the relevant matter if 'it is necessary to avoid prejudice to the prevention, detection or investigation of a criminal offence'. An employer will also be required to inform the employee or worker of the outcome of any investigation undertaken at the conclusion of the investigation.

Lastly, the PDAA introduces a provision whereby an employee or worker will not be liable to any civil, criminal or disciplinary proceedings for making a disclosure which is 'prohibited by any other law, oath, contract, practice or agreement requiring him or her to maintain confidentiality or otherwise restricting the disclosure of the information with respect to a matter'. This provision applies to the disclosure of information that a criminal offence has been committed, is being committed or is likely to be committed or which shows or tends to show that a substantial contravention of, or failure to comply with the law has occurred, is occurring or is likely to occur. This exclusion of liability does not extend to the civil or criminal liability of the employee or worker for his or her participation in the disclosed impropriety.

16.2. Checklist of Do's and Don'ts

- Have established procedures for employees or workers to report irregularities in the workplace so that employees or workers are obliged to follow these procedures if they want to claim protection. This enables the employer to retain an element of control over the process and manage any adverse publicity.
- Integrate whistleblowing policies and procedures with other related policies such as fraud policies, codes of ethics and disciplinary codes. Often these different policies fall under the control or responsibility of different departments and then contradict or conflict with each other, or are unnecessarily voluminous and repetitive.
- Provide for the possibility of anonymous reporting (such as a fraud service hotline) so that even where employees or workers are wary of disclosing their identity, irregular activity is reported.
- Set up procedures for how managers should deal with reports so that reports are properly investigated and irregularities are dealt with.
- Remember that in some instances there are additional reporting obligations on the employer to report certain irregular activities (such as fraud or corruption) to the relevant authorities.
- Make it a disciplinary offence for managers or supervisors to retaliate against employees or workers who make reports.

17. PROHIBITION OF DISCRIMINATION IN THE WORKPLACE

17.1. Overview of Anti-discrimination Laws

The main law regulating discrimination in South Africa is the Constitution. Other laws of relevance include the LRA, the EEA and the PEPUDA.

The preamble of the Constitution states that the aim is 'to establish a society based on democratic values, social justice and fundamental rights' in which 'every citizen is equally protected by the law'. The Constitution outlaws discrimination on grounds such as race, gender, sex, pregnancy, marital status, ethnic or social origin, colour, sexual orientation, age, disability, religion, conscience, belief, culture, language and birth.

One of the most important pieces of legislation enacted with the aim of eliminating unfair discriminatory practices in the workplace is the EEA. The EEA sets out to achieve substantive equality by promoting equal opportunity and fair treatment in employment through the elimination of unfair discrimination. It also implements affirmative action measures to redress the disadvantages in employment experienced by designated groups, in order to ensure their equitable representation in all occupational categories and levels in the workforce.

The EEA places a duty on every employer to eliminate unfair discrimination in its policies and practices.

Much like the Constitution, the EEA contains a general prohibition on unfair discrimination, on one or more of the following grounds: race, gender, sex, pregnancy, marital status, family responsibility, ethnic or social origin, colour, sexual orientation, age, disability, religion, HIV status, conscience, belief, political opinion, culture, language, birth or any other arbitrary ground.

The LRA also contains provisions prohibiting unfair discrimination in the workplace. It is automatically unfair to dismiss an employee on prohibited grounds similar to those contained in the Constitution and the EEA.

PEPUDA is a general anti-discrimination law which is accessible to any person who believes that they have been a victim of discrimination in the broader South African society. It may be used by employees trying to hold their employers liable for alleged acts of discrimination in the employment context in circumstances where specific labour legislation does not adequately cover their complaint. The use of PEPUDA for this purpose is, however, limited in that it only applies to the extent that the EEA is not applicable, for example, in the case of workplace bullying.

Both the Constitution and PEPUDA make a distinction between discrimination and the fairness of the discrimination. Only discrimination which is *unfair* is prohibited.

The Employment Equity Amendment Act No. 47 of 2013 came into effect on 1 August 2014. The central amendments include *inter alia* the following:

(1) The definition given to 'designated groups' has been amended so that beneficiaries of affirmative action are now limited to persons who were citizens of South Africa before 1994 and to their descendants or

to those who would have been entitled to citizenship if apartheid policies had not been enacted.

(2) A new and highly important provision which provides for 'equal pay for work of equal value' which deals with unfair discrimination by employers in respect of terms and conditions of employment of employees doing the same work, similar work or work of equal value.

(3) Strengthening compliance and enforcement mechanisms so that labour inspectors may issue compliance orders that may result in non-complying employers being referred directly to the Labour Court for a fine.

(4) Arising out of the LAC decision in *New Way Motor & Diesel Engineering (Pty) Ltd v. Marsland* [2009] 12 BLLR 1181, an additional ground of discrimination has been provided by the legislation in terms of section 6(1) of the EEA. In terms of this provision, an employee may allege that the employee has been discriminated against on any of the grounds listed in section 6(1), or *on any other arbitrary ground.* The word 'arbitrary' denotes the absence of reason or, at the very least, the absence of a justifiable reason or a ground which is capricious (i.e., impulsive, fickle, erratic, etc.) or a ground that proceeds merely from a whim and is not based on reason or principle or a ground that is purposeless, particularly where the ground impairs or impugns the dignity of an employee who is a member of a group. The meaning attributed to the word 'arbitrary' has recently been confirmed by the Labour Court in *Pioneer Foods (Pty) Ltd v. Workers Against Regression (WAR) & Others* (Case No: C 687/15, 19 April 2016). In this judgment, the Labour Court defined an unfair, arbitrary ground as capricious or for no good reason, and as one that undermines an individual's human dignity.

(5) In the Constitutional Court decision of *Mbana v. Shepstone and Wylie* (CCT85/14) [2015] ZACC 11; 2015 (6) BCLR 693 (CC); (2015) 36 ILJ 1805 (CC) (7 May 2015) the Court noted that, once an allegation of unfair discrimination based on any of the listed grounds in section 6 of the EEA is made, section 11 of the EEA places the burden of proof on the employer to prove that such discrimination did not take place or that it is justified. Where discrimination is alleged on an arbitrary ground, the burden is on the complainant to prove that the conduct complained of is not rational, that it amounts to discrimination and that the discrimination is unfair. The court further held that an employer might be justified in its discrimination where such discrimination is on the basis of the employer's operational requirements. In *Sethole and Others v. Dr Kenneth Kaunda District Municipality* [2018] 1 BLLR (LC) the court found that the employee had not sufficiently discharged their onus in proving discrimination on

an arbitrary ground and accordingly granted the employer absolution from the instance.

(6) The Amendments further saw the introduction of increased arbitration powers at the CCMA which will allow employees an option of referring unfair discrimination cases for CCMA arbitration in the following two circumstances:
   - where there are allegations of sexual harassment on a prescribed ground; and
   - where employees earn less than the earnings threshold.

(7) In this regard, the CCMA's powers were confirmed in the Labour Court judgement of *Famous Brands Management Company (Pty) Ltd v. Commission for Conciliation, Mediation and Arbitration* [2016] 12 BLLR 1217 (LC). In this case, 632 employees referred an unfair discrimination dispute to the CCMA on the basis of unequal pay for equal work. At the hearing, the employer disputed that the CCMA had the jurisdiction to hear and deal with the matter as it was a collective dispute. In this instance, all the employees earned below the earnings threshold and relied on section 10(6)(aA) of EEA to refer the dispute to arbitration at the CCMA as opposed to the Labour Court. This specific section in the EEA allows an employee who earns below the threshold to choose whether to refer the dispute to the Labour Court or to the CCMA. The employer argued that the wording of the section is in the singular, and accordingly it only applies if the dispute involves a single employee. The Commissioner found that the CCMA did in fact have jurisdiction to deal with the dispute. The Commissioners ruling was taken on review to the Labour Court. The Labour Court dismissed the review application. The Judge, in this case, was of the view that the intention of the legislature was to provide an option to all employees who earn below the threshold to refer unfair discrimination disputes to the CCMA in order for the dispute to be dealt in a cost-effective manner. The Court noted that equal pay for equal work claim may be just as complex for one employee as for many employees and that the complexity of the matter does not increase merely because the number of claimants does.

(8) Increased fines and penalties for non-compliance with the EEA which will be linked to the employer's annual turnover (as opposed to profit), and can be as much as 10% of turnover.

(9) In July 2014, section 8 of the EEA was amended to prohibit psychological tests and similar assessments that had not been certified by the Health Professions Council. However, in *Association of Test Publishers of South Africa v. President of the Republic of South Africa & Others* [2017] JOL 39169 it was determined that the amendment

required the highest standard of compliance and yet no framework for certification had been provided. Accordingly, the court declared the amendment null and void.

17.2. Age Discrimination

Under the LRA, a dismissal is automatically unfair if the reason for the dismissal is related to the age of the employee. However, a dismissal based on age is fair if the employee has reached the normal or agreed retirement age for persons employed in that capacity.

The EEA lists 'age' as a prohibited ground, and it has been held that the effect of the EEA, interpreted in compliance with the International Labour Organization Convention 111 and the Constitution, 'is to prohibit age discrimination absolutely'. *See Hospersa obo Venter v. South Africa Nursing Council* [2006] 6 BLLR 558 LC at 32. Therefore, an unjustifiable failure to hire an individual based purely on his or her age constitutes age discrimination. An employer is entitled to select, exclude or differentiate between employees on the basis of their age should such selection, exclusion or differentiation be justified on the basis of the inherent requirements of the job, for example, a youthful film role or if a person has reached the ordinary or usual retirement age in the employers' industry.

17.3. Race Discrimination

The EEA prohibits direct and indirect discrimination based on race. Direct race discrimination occurs where a person is treated differently because of his race or on the basis of some characteristic specific to members of that race. Indirect race discrimination occurs when criteria, conditions or policies are applied which appear to be neutral, but which adversely affect a disproportionate number of a certain race group in circumstances that are not justifiable.

In South African law, a dismissal on the grounds of race is automatically unfair in terms of the LRA and can result in reinstatement plus back pay or up to twenty-four months' remuneration as compensation. The principles applicable to sexual harassment do, however, apply to a large extent to other forms of harassment, including racial discrimination, otherwise referred to as racial harassment.

In *Biggar v. City of Johannesburg (Emergency Management Services)* [2017] JOL 39192 (LC), the applicant alleged unfair discrimination against his employer due to its failure to prevent or sanction numerous acts of racism endured from colleagues. The court found that an employer may be directly responsible in terms of EEA for the creation or tolerance of a racially hostile work environment, which itself is the product of individual acts of a racially discriminatory nature, whether it is committed by persons under the employer's direct control or not. This responsibility stems from the duty of an employer to take steps to ensure that its workplace is free of all forms of racial discrimination. Thus, omissions on the part of the employer to act reasonably and decisively in instances of racism in the workplace may constitute discriminatory conduct.

In this specific case, the employer was ordered, among other things, within fourteen days of the date of the judgment, to pay the employee an amount of two month's salary for failing to take necessary and reasonably practicable steps to prevent him being subjected to racial harassment, and one month's salary for unfairly discriminating against him in taking disciplinary action against him alone, without charging the white complainants.

In *Sasol Chemical Operations (Pty) Ltd v. the CCMA* [2019] 1 BLLR 91 (LC), an employee referred a dispute to the CCMA on the basis that he had received a lower salary than another employee employed in the same position as him, and sought the same salary that was paid to his co-worker. The CCMA found that this was in fact an equal-work-for-equal-pay dispute as envisaged in the EEA and determined that this constituted unfair discrimination on the grounds of race as the applicant employee was black and his co-worker, who earned the higher salary, was white. On review, the Labour Court found that the employee did not allege that the pay inequity was due to racial grounds and that the CCMA was not at liberty to create that case for the applicant employee. The Labour Court confirmed that an employee alleging unfair discrimination on the basis of race bears the evidentiary burden of proving differentiation and that the differentiation was causally connected to the race of the two employees concerned.

17.4. Sex Discrimination/Sexual Harassment

Sexual harassment of an employee is a form of unfair discrimination and is prohibited by the EEA. The EEA contains a Code of Good Practice on the Handling of Sexual Harassment Cases (the 'Code') in the workplace, which provides guidelines for employers, and encourages employers to adopt sexual harassment policies and to communicate those policies to all employees. The Code suggests that the following statements be included in a sexual harassment policy:

- sexual harassment is a form of unfair discrimination on the basis of sex and/or gender and/or sexual orientation which infringes the rights of the complainant and constitutes a barrier to equity in the workplace;
- sexual harassment in the workplace will not be permitted or condoned;
- complainants in sexual harassment matters have the right to follow the procedures in the policy, and appropriate action must be taken by the employer;
- it will be a disciplinary offence to victimize or retaliate against an employee who in good faith lodges a complaint of sexual harassment.

The Code says that the procedures to be followed by a complainant and by an employer when sexual harassment has occurred should be outlined in the policy. In practice, many employers include racial harassment in their policies along with sexual harassment.

It is important to note the recent LAC decision in *Campbell Scientific Africa (Pty) Ltd v. Simmers and Others* [2016] 1 BLLR 1 (LAC). In this judgment, the LAC found that although sexual harassment did not take place in the workplace between co-employees and that the perpetrator had no power or influence over the complainant, it nevertheless amounted to a violation of the complainant's right to dignity and equality.

Further, in *Liberty Group Ltd M* (2017) 38 ILJ 1318 (LAC), the court determined that a sensible meaning must be given to the requirement to report sexual harassment immediately. A court will be satisfied that an employee reported the incident within sufficient time with reference to the facts of each matter. *Rustenburg Platinum Mines Limited v. UASA OBO Steve Pieterson & Others* (JR641/2016) [2018] ZALCJHB 72 followed similar reasoning by noting that in most cases it may 'take ages for the complainant to finally muster the strength and courage to report the incidents' for a myriad of reasons. Thus, the length of time between the incident and the reporting of the same will not have a significant bearing on an employee's claim relating to sexual harassment in the workplace.

Gender discrimination is one of the automatically unfair listed grounds for dismissal in terms of the LRA and is prohibited in terms of the EEA in respect of both employees and candidates for employment.

17.5. Handicap and Disability Discrimination

The EEA prohibits unfair discrimination in the workplace based on a person's disability. The EEA also states that past disadvantages of people with disabilities need to be redressed through affirmative action measures.

Disability is defined in the EEA to mean 'a long-term or recurring physical or mental impairment, which substantially limits their prospects of entry into, or advancement in, employment'.

The Code of Good Practice on the Employment of People with Disabilities (the 'Disability Code') is a guide for employers and employees on how to provide equal opportunities and fair treatment to people with disabilities. The Disability Code applies to both physical and mental disabilities, and requires employers to 'reasonably accommodate the needs of people with disabilities' with the aim of 'reducing the impact of the impairment of the person's capacity to fulfil the essential functions of a job'. The duty arises equally where the disability is voluntarily disclosed by the employee and where it is 'reasonably self-evident' to the employer, and also applies to applicants for employment. However, the duty is not absolute, and an employer should not be required to place an 'unjustifiable hardship' on itself, having regard to the factual situation of the particular employer.

The LRA also protects employees against unfair dismissal on the basis of the employee's disability by declaring such a dismissal to be automatically unfair.

In *Smith v. The Kit Kat Group (Pty) Ltd* [2016] 12 BLLR 1239 (LC), an employee alleged that he was unfairly discriminated against when the employer refused to allow him to return to work for 'cosmetically unacceptable' reasons. In this case, the employee had attempted suicide, which resulted in a deformity to his face and an impairment to his speech. Following the suicide attempt, the employee was granted time off by the employer in order to recover and was told that he could return to work at a later stage. The employee sometime later, requested to return to work but was told by the employer that his facial appearance was not acceptable and that it would remind employees of the attempted suicide. It was proposed by the employer that the employee lodge a disability claim against the provident fund. The employee decided against lodging such a claim in fear that it might amount to fraud given that the disability was self-inflicted. A meeting was held between the employee and the employer where the employee was not formally dismissed but was told that he could not return to work for cosmetic reasons. In this case, the Judge was of the view that it was clear that the employee had a disability as defined in the EEA. The Judge was further of the view that the employer also considered the employee to have a disability given their suggestion that the employee lodge a disability claim. The Court found that while the Code of Good Practice: Dismissal provides that an employer need not accommodate an employee with a disability if it would impose unjustifiable hardship, it would not have constituted unjustifiable hardship to permit the employee to return to work and attempt to prove that he could perform his duties. In the event that he could not perform them satisfactorily, then the employer could proceed with an incapacity process. The fact that the employer just refused to allow the employee to return to work amounted to discrimination on the grounds of disability. The court awarded damages equal to twenty-four months' remuneration, and a further six months compensation as solatium due to the fact that the employee had suffered humiliation.

In the Labour Court judgment of *Jansen v. Legal Aid South Africa* (2018) 39 ILJ 2024 (LC), the employee referred an automatically unfair dismissal dispute, claiming that the true reason for his dismissal was his disability. The employee had been diagnosed with, and was treated for, clinical depression and anxiety, which caused him to act erratically and aggressively and made him unable to attend work on many occasions. His employer was aware of his mental illness. However, he was charged with various allegations of misconduct, including absence without permission, insolence and refusal to obey a lawful and reasonable instruction, and he was ultimately dismissed. The Labour Court found that the employee's mental illness was the true cause of his dismissal as the mental illness had caused the employee to act in the way that he did. In the circumstances, the Labour Court found that the employer was under the obligation to reasonably accommodate him in the workplace, which it had failed to do. The employee was reinstated with full retrospective effect and was awarded compensation amounting to his six months' salary.

17.6. National Origin Discrimination

Discrimination on the basis of a person's social or ethnic origin is expressly prohibited by section 6(1) of the EEA. The PEPUDA prohibits such discrimination against persons who are not job applicants or employees.

17.7. Religious Discrimination

Section 15 of the Constitution provides everyone with the right to freedom of conscience, religion, thought, belief and opinion. The EEA also prohibits discrimination against employees or applicants for employment on the grounds of religion. As far as possible, reasonable accommodation is required in order to respect an employee's religion. Religion does not constitute a 'designated group' which must be reasonably accommodated in the EEA. Nevertheless, it will be difficult for an employer to justify a refusal to accommodate an employee's religious practices insofar as such accommodation would be reasonable. Examples of reasonable accommodation in practice include the provision of prayer rooms and allowing longer lunch breaks for Muslim employees to accommodate Friday prayers. Certain employers also provide for one or more days of religious holiday leave annually.

In the 2006 case of *Dlamini v. Green Four Security* (2006) 27 ILJ 2098 (LC), a number of security guards were dismissed for failing to adhere to the company policy to be clean-shaven. They were members of the Baptized Nazareth Group and alleged that their religion did not permit them to shave or trim their beards. The Labour Court held that they had to prove that shaving their beards was prohibited as an essential tenet of their faith. The company applied its policy consistently to all employees, and there was no proof of discrimination on account of religious beliefs. In the circumstances, the Labour Court found that applicants were not discriminated against, and accordingly, their dismissal was not unfair. In *Department of Correctional Services and Another v. Police and Prisons Civil Rights Union and Others* (2013) 34 ILJ 1375 (SCA), however, the Supreme Court of Appeal held that a workplace policy was not justified if it restricted a practice of religious belief or a cultural belief that did not affect an employee's ability to perform his duties, nor jeopardize the safety of the public or other employees, nor cause undue hardship to the employer in a practical sense.

In the recent LAC judgment of *TDF Network Africa (Pty) Ltd v. Faris* [2019] 2 BLLR 127 (LAC), the Court was required to determine whether the dismissal of an employee due to incapacity constituted an automatically unfair dismissal, on the grounds of religion. The employee in question was a practising Seventh Day Adventist. Her religion prohibited her from partaking in secular labour on Saturdays, with exceptions made for emergency humanitarian work. The employer, for various sound operational requirements, conducted its stock take on Saturdays and insisted that the employee attends at work to assist with the stock take. The employee refused and was dismissed on the grounds of incapacity. The LAC held that the employer bears the burden of proving that it is impossible to accommodate the individual employee without imposing undue hardship or insurmountable operational difficulty. There was no evidence placed before the Court to indicate that the employer had suffered any hardship from the employee's absence at work on Saturdays. The LAC held that an employment practice that penalizes an employee for practising her religion is a palpable invasion of her dignity in that it supposes that her religion is not worthy of protection or respect. In the circumstances, the LAC found that the employee's dismissal was automatically unfair and awarded her twelve months' compensation.

17.8. Military Status Discrimination

Military Status is not a protected class under the Constitution or the EEA. In fact, members of the South African National Defence Force, National Intelligence Agency, the South African Secret Service, the South African National Academy of Intelligence and the directors and staff of Comsec are excluded from the operation of the LRA and EEA.

If an employee or a job applicant is discriminated against on the basis of their military status, such a person could possibly argue that they have been discriminated against on an arbitrary ground, that is, there is no rational justification for such distinction.

17.9. Pregnancy Discrimination

The EEA lists 'pregnancy' as a prohibited ground of discrimination. It defines pregnancy as including 'intended pregnancy, termination of pregnancy and any medical circumstances related to pregnancy'. Pursuant to the LRA, a dismissal based on pregnancy, intended pregnancy or a reason related to pregnancy is automatically unfair.

In the context of maternity leave, the provisions of the BCEA refer specifically to an 'employee' and not necessarily to a 'female employee'. In the most recent case on the subject, *M I A v. State Information Technology Agency (Pty) Ltd* (D 312/2012) [2015] ZALCD 20; 2015 (6) SA 250 (LC); [2015] 7 BLLR 694 (LC); (2015) 36 ILJ 1905 (LC) (26 March 2015) the Labour Court held that a man in a same-sex marriage in terms of the Civil Union Act No. 17 of 2006, was entitled to four months' maternity leave, in circumstances where he and his spouse had concluded a surrogacy agreement with the surrogate mother, where the surrogate mother would immediately hand over the child to him and his spouse at the birth of the child, and where he and his spouse had agreed that he would perform the role ordinarily performed by the birth mother. Employers must make provision for such employees to take maternity leave in terms of the BCEA or in terms of its leave policy.

Section 26 of the BCEA provides protection to employees before and after the birth of a child and prohibits employers from requiring or permitting pregnant employees or those nursing their children to perform work that is hazardous to their health or the health of their child. Further, during the pregnancy and for a period of six months after the birth, the employer must offer suitable, alternative employment. In *Manyetsa v. New Kleinfontein Gold Mine (Pty) Ltd* (2018) 39 ILJ 415 (LC) the court considered whether removing an employee from her normal workstation and placing her on extended unpaid maternity leave as opposed to placing her in an alternative position amounted to discrimination. The court found that failure to place the employee in alternative position did not amount to discrimination in this instance as 'suitable alternative employment' involves an assessment of whether that position is capable of being a suitable position for that particular employee. Hence, where 'suitable alternative work' cannot be secured, the employer may not have acted unfairly.

17.10. Marital Status Discrimination

According to the Constitution and the EEA, no person may unfairly discriminate, directly or indirectly, against an employee, in any employment policy or practice on the basis of that employee's marital status. It has been held that marital status is closely related to human dignity and freedom and that discrimination on the basis of marital status infringes human dignity and worth of the individual in the same way as other recognized grounds of discrimination. (*Volks v. Robinson* (2009) JDR 1018 (CC). *See also Daniels v. Campbell No and Others* (2004) (5) SA 331 (CC)).

17.11. Sexual Orientation Discrimination

The Constitution outlaws discrimination on the basis of sexual orientation.

The EEA also prohibits discrimination against employees or applicants for employment on the basis of their sexual orientation. The South African courts have, in numerous cases, upheld the right of gay and lesbian persons not to be discriminated against on the basis of their sexual orientation (*see,* e.g., *National Coalition for Gay and Lesbian Equality & Another v. Minister of Justice & Others* [1998] 3 All SA 26 (W) and *Atkins v. Datacentrix (Pty) Ltd* [2010] 4 BLLR 351 (LC)). The courts have also ruled that the Marriage Act is unconstitutional insofar as it does not make provision for the rights of people in permanent same-sex relationships (*Fourie and Another v. Minister of Home Affairs and Others* [2005] 1 All SA 273 (SCA)). In 2006, the Civil Union Act No. 17 of 2006 was enacted to regulate the solemnization and registration of civil unions by way of either a marriage or a civil partnership and to provide for the legal consequences of the solemnization and consequences of registration of civil unions.

Same-sex spouses are able to obtain dependant visa status provided that they are married or have been in a life partnership for a minimum period of two years.

17.12. Equal Work for Equal Pay

The new amendments of the EEA prescribe that a difference in terms and conditions of employment between employees of the same employer performing the same or substantially the same work or work of equal value that is directly or indirectly based on one or more of the listed grounds is unfair discrimination.

To establish pay discrimination, it is necessary for the complainant to show that the work performed by the complainant is equal or of equal value to that of a more highly remunerated comparator and such difference in pay is based on a prohibited ground of discrimination. The complainant would need to prove that the differentiation is primarily as a result of the alleged ground for discrimination (*South African Municipal Workers Union and Another v. Nelson Mandela Bay Municipality* [2016] 2 BLLR 202 (LC)).

In *Pioneer Foods (Pty) Ltd v. Workers Against Regression (WAR) & Others* (Case No. C-687/15, 19 April 2016), the court stated that in order to prove that the conduct complained of amounts to unfair discrimination, the complainant must identify the listed or unlisted arbitrary ground of discrimination relied upon, establish that the ground is an arbitrary ground and prove that the ground is the reason for the disparate treatment complained of.

In light of the above case authority, it may be difficult for a complainant to prove that he or she has been unfairly discriminated against on the basis of an arbitrary ground. In the circumstances, it may be prudent for the complainant to possibly pursue an unfair labour practice claim in terms of section 186(2)(a) of the LRA on the basis that the employer acted unfairly in respect of the provision of benefits. In *Apollo Tyres South Africa (Pty) Ltd v. Commission for Conciliation, Mediation and Arbitration and Others* [2013] 5 BLLR 434 (LAC), the LAC defined a benefit as an existing advantage or privilege to which an employee is entitled as a right or granted in terms of a policy or practice subject to the employer's discretion. Given the broad definition of a benefit, a complainant may have greater prospects of succeeding with an unfair practice claim as opposed to equal pay for equal work claims. This is particularly so when no unfair discrimination is present or likely to be established.

17.13. Retaliation

The LRA says that no person may take negative action against an employee (or a person seeking employment) for exercising any right conferred by that Act. In addition, no person may give an advantage, or promise to give an advantage to an employee or a person seeking employment in exchange for that person not exercising any right conferred by the Act or not participating in any proceedings under the Act.

The Code of Good Practice on the Handling of Sexual Harassment Cases also provides that it will be a disciplinary offence to victimize or retaliate against an employee who in good faith lodges a complaint of sexual harassment. There are similar protections in the BCEA in relation to rights conferred by the BCEA.

17.14. Constructive Discharge

Constructive dismissal occurs where an employee resigns because the employer has breached a fundamental term of the employee's contract of employment or has made the employee's work intolerable so as to render continued employment impossible. Discriminatory conduct by an employer may form the factual basis of a constructive dismissal claim. Such a dismissal is considered automatically unfair under the LRA and may give rise to up to twenty-four months compensation in terms of the LRA. Reinstatement and backpay are not normally awarded or sought in a constructive dismissal case.

17.15. Checklist of Do's and Don'ts

- Ensure that any criteria, conditions or policies which appear to be neutral do not adversely affect members of a certain group as this could amount to indirect discrimination.
- Immediately investigate any complaint of discrimination lodged by an employee and take the necessary action to remedy the situation.
- Do not take into consideration arbitrary considerations such as race, religion, marital status, etc., when making decisions in respect of employees or applicants for employment unless there is a legal justification for so doing.
- Do not retaliate against an employee who in good faith lodges a complaint of discrimination.

18. SMOKING IN THE WORKPLACE

18.1. Overview

Smoking in the workplace is regulated by the Tobacco Products Control Act No. 83 of 1993, the Tobacco Products Control Amendment Act No. 23 of

2007 and the Tobacco Products Control Amendment Act No. 63 of 2008 which came into effect on 21 August 2009. Together, these laws provide that smoking is prohibited in any public place, which means any indoor, enclosed or partially enclosed area that is open to the public or any part of the public. This includes workplace and public transportation. A workplace is defined as:

- any indoor, enclosed or partially enclosed area in which employees perform the duties of their employment; and
- any corridor, lobby, stairwell, elevator, cafeteria, washroom or other common area frequented by employees during the course of their employment.

The recent regulations also provide that no person may smoke any tobacco product within a 10 m distance from a window of, ventilation inlet of, the doorway to or entrance into a public place.

A workplace does not include any private dwelling and any designated smoking area that complies with certain prescribed requirements, even if the designated area would normally be classified as part of a workplace. If the workplace is considered to be a public place (as per the definition set out above), the employer may designate a specific portion of the workplace as a smoking area. Employees who do smoke are then able to smoke on the premises, while still protecting the non-smoking employees.

There is no definition for 'partially enclosed'. However, it seems clear that where there is only one side open (such as on a covered balcony and/or in a courtyard and/or partially enclosed parking area), this will constitute a 'partially enclosed' area, and smoking is prohibited. Thus, it is best practice for employers not to allow smoking on the balconies of their buildings or in the parking area if it is partially enclosed.

A designated smoking area has to conform to certain requirements, including that it may not exceed 25% of the total floor area of the workplace, must be separated from the rest of the workplace by a solid partition, must have ventilation that ensures that the air from the smoking area is directly exhausted to the outside and must display certain prescribed messages and/or signs.

All employers are required to have a written policy on smoking in the workplace. This policy should have been prepared and applied in the workplace by no later than 1 January 2001. The employer is also required to display signs and make announcements (e.g., in its internal policies and rules, during induction of employees and the like) that smoking, other than in designated smoking areas, is prohibited. Employers have a duty to ensure that smoking laws are followed. An employer is required by law to ensure that:

- no person smokes anywhere other than a designated smoking area;
- employees who do not want to be exposed to tobacco smoke in the workplace are protected from tobacco smoke in that workplace;
- employees may object to tobacco smoke in the workplace without retaliation of any kind;
- it is not a condition of employment, express or implied, that any employee is required to work in any portion of the workplace where smoking is permitted; and
- employees are not required to sign any indemnity for working in any portion of the workplace where smoking is permitted.

If employers do not ensure that the laws are complied with, they may also face a fine or possible imprisonment. The fines were increased under the amendments to a maximum of ZAR 1,000,000 for certain contraventions. Employees could also take action against the employer based on its failure to create a safe and healthy working environment.

On 9 May 2018, the Draft Control of Tobacco Products and Electronic Systems Bill was published for public comment. The Bill aims to address the changes that technology has brought to the industry, with particular reference to vapes, e-cigarettes and other kinds of electronic nicotine delivery systems. While the Bill has not yet been passed into law, should it be enacted, employers will be under an obligation to manage any electronic delivery system in the same manner as any other tobacco product.

Amongst others, an employer must ensure that: (a) employees who do not want to be exposed to smoke are not exposed; (b) it is not a condition of employment that employees are required to work in a workplace area where smoking is legally permitted; and (c) employees are not required to sign any indemnity for working in any portion of the workplace where smoking is permitted by law.

18.2. Checklist of Do's and Don'ts

- Have a written smoking policy in place.
- Make sure that the designated smoking area complies with the legislation in terms of size and specifications.
- Post signs telling employees and other people who enter the premises that smoking is prohibited.
- make it a disciplinary offence to contravene the smoking policy and inform your employees about the policy when they join the business.
- Do not allow smoking in areas that could be classified as partially enclosed.

– Do not retaliate against employees who raise objections to exposure to tobacco smoke.

19. USE OF DRUGS AND ALCOHOL IN THE WORKPLACE

19.1. OVERVIEW

An employer is entitled to require that employees not drink alcohol or use drugs at work or to require that they not be under the influence of drugs or alcohol while at work (even if not consumed at the workplace), but employees are entitled to do as they please away from work and on their own time.

Any medical testing that is conducted by the employer is subject to the rights and freedoms guaranteed to job applicants and employees by the Constitution. Employees have the right to equality, human dignity, freedom and security of the person and privacy. The Labour Court has[12] held that the core rights affected are the rights everyone has to bodily and psychological integrity, which includes the right to security in and control over their body and the right not to be subjected to medical or scientific experiments without their informed consent. The exercise of these core rights is also an exercise of one's inherent right to dignity. The right to physical integrity includes the right of a person to control their body by consenting or not consenting to or subjecting or not subjecting their body to any treatment, tests, experiment, or any other physical, mental or psychological experience. The right is infringed by conduct that causes physical pain, mental distress, shock, loss of life expectancy, loss of amenities of life, inconvenience and discomfort, disability and disfigurement. The court cited medical interventions as an example of conduct that amounts to the infringement of the right.

This means that employers cannot force employees to undergo testing for alcohol and drugs, even if they have given consent to such testing at some earlier stage (usually in the employment contract). If, however, the employee has consented to testing in the contract, while the employer cannot force the test, he can discipline the employee for breach of contract. The employer can also rely on observational evidence of the employee being under the influence of drugs or alcohol at the workplace, such as slurred speech, unsteadiness, the smell of alcohol on the employee's breath, etc., although this is of course less reliable than proper scientific testing. Where testing is of importance to the employer, it is a good idea to include consent to testing in the contract. Another way of doing testing would be via a collective agreement with the union.

The EEA provides in section 7 that:

12. *PFG Building Glass (Pty) Ltd v. CEPPAWU & Others* [2003] 5 BLLR 475 (LC).

> Medical testing of an employee is prohibited, unless –
> (a) the legislation permits or requires the testing; or
> (b) it is justifiable in the light of medical facts, employment conditions, social policy, the fair distribution of employee benefits or the inherent requirements of a job.

However, as with all constitutional rights, the rights of the employee which would tend to prevent testing are not absolute. They can be limited in appropriate circumstances. Medical testing is sometimes required by health and safety law. For example, OHSA and the Mine Health & Safety Act require an employer to provide, as far as reasonably practical, a safe workplace. Medical testing in hazardous workplace environments facilitates both the identification of employees that are susceptible to or have been exposed to the risk of other dangerous substances, injuries or diseases and the adoption of protective measures and the minimizing of any harmful effects.

Further, where an employee returns to work following an illness or injury, testing may indicate whether the employee is still able to discharge the inherent requirements of the job, whether there is a need for job restructuring, reassignment or some other assistance so that the employee can be reasonably accommodated in the workplace. It is arguable that where there are reasonable grounds to believe that the employee, because of health reasons, is no longer capable of discharging the inherent requirements of the job or poses a danger to health and safety in the workplace it would be legitimate to require medical testing as part of assessing the employee's fitness for work.

Queries relating to an applicant for employment's use of illegal drugs could entail applicants incriminating themselves, and there is no general duty on applicants to disclose prejudicial information to the employer. However, asking an applicant is he or she currently uses illegal drugs would probably be a legitimate question given the employer's legitimate interest in employing someone who is not a substance abuser, particularly where the inherent requirements of the job dictate this (e.g., because the employee will be working in a hazardous environment or with dangerous machinery).

The fact that an applicant for employment drinks alcohol outside of work would not be a good reason not to hire him or her, and it would probably constitute unfair discrimination on an arbitrary (rather than a specifically listed) ground unless the employer could prove inherent requirements of the job.

In a recent case, *Minister of Justice and Constitutional Development and Others v. Prince and Others* [2018] JOL 40399 (CC), it was held by the Constitutional Court that the personal use of cannabis in private by an individual is not unlawful. Employers in South Africa are now grappling with how to deal with determining whether employees who have used cannabis lawfully outside working hours in private are affected by this while at work.

Where testing does take place, the confidentiality of the information must be protected. That duty rests on any person designated by the employer to administer or safeguard any confidential information acquired in the conducting of any medical test. Section 59 of the EEA provides that any person who discloses any confidential information acquired in the performance of a function under the EEA commits an offence, unless the information is needed to allow a person to perform a function under the EEA, or the information must be disclosed by law.

The Immigration Act and regulations provide that medical and radiological reports must be submitted to the Department of Home Affairs in support of temporary and permanent residence visa applications.

19.2. Checklist of Do's and Don'ts

- Establish written policies and provisions in employment contracts requiring employees' consent to testing for drugs or alcohol if regular or random testing will be done. Bear in mind that employees can still refuse to take the test, but if your clause if appropriately worded, the employee can then be disciplined for breach of contract.
- Have carefully worded disciplinary codes that describe the various offences involving drug or alcohol abuse. They should cover both possession and being under the influence and can include the specific offence of having a blood alcohol content that is over a specified limit.
- Avoid offences that are too technical, as these can be difficult to prove.
- Providing a checklist for managers to complete when employees are observed to be under the influence of alcohol or drugs at work.
- Have protocols and procedures dealing with what to do if an employee is apparently under the influence and not fit to work.
- Have a policy on how to deal with employees who admit that they have a drug or alcohol dependency problem, and who raise this as a defence to disciplinary infractions.
- Do not force employees to submit to drug or alcohol testing against their will, even if they have agreed to testing in their employment contracts. Instead, discipline them for breach of contract.
- Do not allow employees to work, especially with dangerous machinery or hazardous substances, if they are apparently under the influence and may pose a health and safety risk to themselves or others.

20. AIDS, HIV, SARS, BLOOD-BORNE PATHOGENS

20.1. Overview

The Constitution does not expressly prohibit discrimination based on AIDS, HIV or other illnesses. However, the Constitutional Court has held that HIV/AIDS can be regarded as analogous to the grounds specifically listed in the Constitution upon which discrimination will prima facie be found to be unfair. The test for unfair discrimination (as set out in *Harksen v. Lane NO and Others* 1997 (11) BCLR 1489 (CC)) is whether the conduct has the potential to impair human dignity.

The EEA specifically provides that employees and applicants for employment may not be discriminated against on the basis of their HIV status. The EEA also regulates the testing of employees to determine their HIV status. Testing of an employee to determine HIV status is prohibited unless such testing is determined justifiable by the Labour Court. Some of the criteria which the Labour Court will consider in determining whether testing is justified include the following:

- testing has to be voluntary and anonymous;
- testing has to be conducted with the consent of the employees and cannot be required as a condition of employment, promotion and/or other benefits;
- the samples have to be received and processed by a reputable and specialized testing company;
- the applicant and its management must not be involved in the testing, apart from participating as employees themselves;
- HIV positive employees should not be discriminated against should the employer become aware of their status;
- the purpose of the testing must only be to discover the percentage of HIV positive employees in order to enable the company to plan an effective HIV/AIDS strategy;
- no prejudicial inference should be drawn from a refusal to submit to testing;
- the employer should not be aware of which employees have undergone such testing.

In authorizing testing for HIV, the Labour Court may make any order it considers appropriate, including imposing conditions relating to:

- the provision of counselling;
- the maintenance of confidentiality;
- the period during which the authorization for any testing applies; and

- the category or categories of jobs or employees in respect of which the authorization for testing applies.

The permission of the Labour Court is, however, not required if HIV testing is requested by an employee.

The EEA provides that any testing for SARS and blood-borne pathogens may only take place if permitted or required by legislation, and if it is justifiable in the light of medical facts, employment conditions, social policy, the fair distribution of employee benefits or the inherent requirements of the job.

Persons infected with or carrying infectious, communicable or other diseases or viruses as prescribed by the Immigration Act and regulations thereto are prohibited persons and do not qualify for a port of entry visa, admission into the Republic, a visa or permanent residence. The diseases or viruses contemplated are those promulgated under the International Health Regulations Act No. 28 of 1974, and any other disease or virus rendering a person inadmissible as may be determined by the Department of Health from time to time in terms of the applicable legislation. The list usually accords with those issued by the World Health Organization. The Director General may, for a good cause, declare such a person not to be a prohibited person.

20.2. Checklist of Do's and Don'ts

(a) Do not enquire about the HIV/AIDS status of an employee or applicant for employment.
(b) Do not conduct HIV testing on employees or job applicants without first getting permission from the Labour Court.
(c) Ensure that HIV positive employees do not suffer any occupational detriment as a result of their status.

21. DRESS AND GROOMING REQUIREMENTS

21.1. Overview

There are no specific laws in South Africa which regulate dress or grooming requirements. However, employers have a legitimate and recognized interest in administering a dress code or grooming standard. Many employers require employees to wear a standard uniform that forms part of the company's image and branding. Where a uniform is not prescribed, employers may place limits on the type of clothes which employees can wear to work or establish general guidelines for what is acceptable and what is not. This normally applies to employees who interact with customers. Such rules need to be supported by reasonable commercial considerations.

Dress codes or grooming standards that limit employees' rights to dress in religious or ethnic garb could possibly give rise to claims of religious discrimination. The same applies where employees are not allowed to grow beards or dreadlocks, as in the LAC judgment of *Department of Correctional Services and Another v. Popcru and Others* [2012] 2 BLLR 110 (LAC). In this case, the Departmental Dress Code prohibited male warders (but not female warders) from dying their hair or cutting it 'in any punk style, including a "Dreadlocks" hairstyle'. Some of the dismissed officers based their claim on the fact that they were members of the Rastafarian religion, asserting that they wore dreadlocks as an outward manifestation of their religion.

The SCA upheld the decision of the LAC that the dismissal of several warders for non-compliance with the Departmental Dress Code was automatically unfair, on the basis that it discriminated against the officers on the basis of religion, culture and gender.

Ultimately the Courts balance the legitimate commercial needs of the employer and the industry in which the employee operates with the employee's rights to dress and groom as the employee pleases, particularly in accordance with religious, cultural and ethnic affiliation.

21.2. Checklist of Do's and Don'ts

- Policies must be reasonable with regard to their specific context.
- Policies must be applied uniformly; inconsistent enforcement can give rise to discrimination claims.
- Do not institute a policy that limits religious or other ethnic dress without considering anti-discrimination laws.
- Do not create a policy that imposes significantly more restrictions on women than men.
- Ensure that dress code and appearance standards are supported by legitimate safety, job performance, or public image concerns.

22. PRIVACY, TECHNOLOGY AND TRANSFER OF PERSONAL DATA

22.1. Privacy Rights of Employees

22.1.1. Overview

In South Africa, everyone (including employees) has a constitutionally guaranteed right to privacy, which includes the right not to have their person or home searched; their property searched, their possessions seized or the privacy of their communications infringed. However, the courts have held (in *Bernstein & Others v. Bester & Others NNO* (1996) (2) SA 751(CC), for example) that the right to privacy relates only to the most personal aspects of a person's existence, and that as a person moves into communal relations and activities such as business (and employment) and social interaction, the scope of personal space shrinks accordingly.

In the workplace, the employer should generally be able to monitor its employees' productivity, investigate misconduct and evaluate the quality of the work produced by the employees. However, the form of such monitoring must always be consistent with the employees' right to privacy – and its limitations – and comply with legislative prescriptions where applicable. Thus, for example, closed-circuit camera surveillance of the loading area of a warehouse where the employees have been warned that there is such surveillance will not infringe the employees' rights to privacy. Such surveillance in the workplace toilets, however, is not likely to be allowed.

As indicated in section 3.3 above, legislation (POPI) regulating data privacy in detail and the processing of personal data of employees has been enacted but is not yet in force. POPI is dealt with in more detail in section 26 below.

The ROICA regulates, amongst other things, the monitoring of usage by employees of an employer's computers, e-mail, telephones, etc. Such monitoring is generally prohibited by ROICA, but the prohibition is subject to certain exceptions, two of which are relevant for present purposes:

- First, such monitoring is permitted if the employer has obtained the prior written consent of the employee to do so.
- Second, such monitoring is permitted in circumstances where the employer does not have the prior written consent, but the monitoring is of communications relating to or occurring during the carrying on of the business. There are a range of factors that must be present when monitoring in this regard, such as: (a) the monitoring must have the consent of the official of the company who has been appointed the 'system controller' for purposes of ROICA; (b) the telecommunication system

concerned must be provided for use wholly or partly in connection with the business; and (c) the system controller must have made all reasonable efforts to inform in advance the employee who uses the telecommunication system concerned that communications transmitted thereby may be monitored.

22.2. Checklist of Do's and Don'ts

- Include ROICA written consent provisions in your contracts of employment and have a written e-mail and communications policy that warns employees that their use of the company phones, e-mail systems and computers may be monitored.
- Assess any methods of processing and monitoring personal information about employees against the right to privacy principles established under POPI.

23. WORKPLACE INVESTIGATIONS FOR COMPLAINTS OF DISCRIMINATION, HARASSMENT, FRAUD, THEFT AND WHISTLEBLOWING

23.1. Overview

The Code of Good Practice on the Handling of Sexual Harassment Cases in the Workplace encourages employers to have a policy and a procedure for handling complaints. This policy must be communicated to all employees. Employers must investigate complaints of harassment brought to their attention and must take all reasonable steps to eliminate the harassment. Failure to do so may result in liability for the employer. This will also be the case where the discrimination was committed by one of its employees, and the employer failed to address the problem when it was brought to its attention.

The LAC in *Liberty Group Ltd v. M* (2017) 38 ILJ 1318 (LAC) held that an employer could be liable for an unfair discrimination claim in terms of section 60 of the EEA No. 55 of 1998 if it fails to take reasonable steps to protect an employee from sexual harassment. In this case, the employee alleged that she was sexually harassed by a fellow employee. The Court emphasized that reasonable steps need to be taken at the earliest opportunity once the sexual harassment has been brought to the employer's attention. In this case, the employer was found liable for unfair discrimination because it failed to take reasonable steps from the first allegation of sexual harassment. Instead, the employer took some form of action once the employee had resigned.

Employers are obliged to report instances of theft and fraud, in excess of a certain amount, which occur in the workplace to the authorities. It is therefore incumbent on employers to properly investigate any instances of fraud and theft in order to be able to comply with this obligation.

Pursuant to the PDA, an employee who has reasonable grounds to believe that he may be adversely affected as a result of making a whistleblowing claim must be transferred to another post or position within the employer's organization, or to another agency of the State, if the State is the employer. This is, however, subject to the qualification that the employee applies for such a transfer and the transfer is reasonably possible or practicable. The PDAA of 2017 now includes the protection of both *employees and workers*, former or current, when they blow the whistle on their employer. This amendment was introduced to allow the Act to encompass independent contractors, consultants, agents and temporary employees. Additionally, the amendment empowers both an employee and a worker to approach the courts for relief where they are subjected to detrimental consequences by their employers. Regulations Relating to Protected Disclosures, 2018, prescribing the persons and bodies to whom an employee or worker may make a protected disclosure and providing descriptions of the matters usually dealt with by the persons and bodies, were made in September 2018.

23.2. Checklist of Do's and Don'ts

- Employers should immediately take reasonable steps to investigate complaints of discrimination and harassment brought to their attention.
- Employers ought to report instances of theft and fraud which occur in the workplace to the authorities and may be legally obliged to do so in terms of the Prevention and Combating of Corrupt Activities Act if the amount involved exceeds ZAR 100,000. A failure to do so constitutes a criminal offence by the employer.
- Employers ought to report suspicious transactions, including when a cash transaction is over a prescribed limit or when the transaction is deemed to be suspicious in terms of the criteria set out by the Financial Intelligence Center Act No. 38 of 2001.
- An employee or worker who blows the whistle on corrupt activities in the workplace should not suffer any occupational detriment as a result.

24. AFFIRMATIVE ACTION/NON-DISCRIMINATION REQUIREMENTS

24.1. Overview

Both the Constitution and the EEA contain provisions relating to affirmative action. Section 9(2) of the Constitution states that 'Equality includes the full and equal enjoyment of all rights and freedoms. To promote the achievement of equality, legislative and other measures designed to protect or advance persons or categories of persons disadvantaged by discrimination may be taken.' It furthermore states that affirmative action is implemented in order to achieve long-term substantive equality. The beneficiaries of affirmative action are identified as 'persons or categories of persons, disadvantaged by unfair discrimination'.

Affirmative action measures must, according to the Constitution, be 'designed to achieve' certain goals. From a substantive perspective, if the measure is applied, it must be clear that substantive equality is both intended and expected, that is, such measures must fairly advance representativity of designated groups (black people, women and people with disabilities). From a procedural perspective, a degree of planning, consideration and rationality must have preceded the implementation of the measure, that is, a properly considered Employment Equity Plan and Affirmative Action Policy are essential.

The EEA places an obligation on every 'designated employer' to implement affirmative action measures. The designated employer is defined to include employers who employ fifty or more employees, and employers who employ less than fifty employees but whose annual turnover at any given time exceeds an amount stipulated in a Schedule to the EEA.

The EEA prescribes affirmative action measures that have to be implemented and those that may be implemented. The EEA also provides for 'Employment Equity Plans' that have to be prepared, submitted to the Director General of the Department of Labour, and implemented and monitored in the workplace. The EEA establishes a variety of enforcement mechanisms to ensure compliance with the EEA. All these provisions assist in ensuring that affirmative action achieves the above purposes.

The EEA designates the beneficiaries of affirmative action as individuals from 'designated groups' who are suitably qualified. A 'designated group' is defined to include 'black people, women and people with disabilities'. 'Black people' is furthermore defined to include 'Africans, Coloureds and Indians'. In terms of a High Court decision, people of Chinese descent are now also included under the term 'coloured'. 'People with disabilities' are 'people who have a long-term physical or mental impairment which substantially limits their prospects of entry into, or advancement in, employment'. A 'suitably qualified person' is defined as a person who may be qualified for a job as a result of any one of, or any combination of, that person's formal qualifications, prior learning, relevant experience, or capacity to acquire, within a reasonable time, the ability to do the job.

A designated employer must prepare and implement an employment equity plan which will achieve reasonable progress towards employment equity in the workplace. The plan should state the objectives to be achieved for each year of the plan. It must also state the affirmative action measures to be implemented. This includes:

- measures to identify and eliminate employment barriers, including unfair discrimination, which adversely affect persons from designated groups;
- measures designed to further diversify the workplace based on equal dignity and respect for people;
- making reasonable accommodation for people from designated groups in order to ensure that they enjoy equal opportunities and are equitably represented in the workplace;
- ensuring the equitable representation of suitably qualified people from designated groups in all occupational categories and levels in the workforce;
- retaining and developing people from designated groups and implementing appropriate training measures.

The importance of an employment equity plan was illustrated in the case of *Solidarity obo Pretorius v. City of Tshwane Metropolitan Municipality and Another* [2016] 7 BLLR 685 (LC). In this case, the municipality admitted that it discriminated against the applicant by failing to consider him for the position as he was not a member of a designated group but argued that this was not unfair as it was permitted to do so under the EEA. The court held that if the municipality had acted in accordance with an employment equity plan when discriminating against the applicant then the discrimination could not have been unfair. The municipality, however, conceded that it did not have an employment equity plan in place at the time that it discriminated against the applicant. It nevertheless argued that it had acted in accordance with its staffing policy contained in a collective agreement and thus this constituted an affirmative action measure under section 15 of the EEA. It was held that the EEA requires employers to have an employment equity plan setting out measurable targets before simply excluding candidates for appointment on the grounds of race or gender. Thus, the exclusion of the applicant, because he was a white male in the absence of an employment equity plan, amounted to unfair discrimination.

Where under-representation of people from designated groups has been identified, the employment equity plan must state the numerical goals to achieve equitable representation of suitably qualified people from designated groups within each category and level in the workforce, the timetable within which this is to be achieved and the strategies intended to achieve these goals.

An employer is required to ensure that each occupational level in its workforce is equitably represented in relation to the demographic profile of the national and regional economically active population, which may adversely affect provinces with large regionally based minorities. In *Solidarity and Others v. Department of Correctional Services and Others* (2016) (5) SA 594 (CC) the Constitutional Court confirmed that where an employer fails to take into account the regional demographics of a particular province in an employment equity plan, the plan would be non-compliant with the EEA.

Employers are required to submit a report to the Director General of the Department of Labour every year detailing the progress which they have made in implementing their employment equity plan.

The Labour Court may impose a fine in accordance with Schedule 1 of the EEA for any contravention of the affirmative action provisions of the EEA. Schedule 1 specifies maximum permissible penalties that may be imposed for contravening the EEA. The current maximum penalty is the greater of ZAR 2.7 million or 10% of the employer's annual turnover, if the employer has previously contravened the same provision within three years.

It must be noted that there is currently an Employment Equity Amendment Bill which is in the process of being made into legislation. This bill intends to fast-track transformation in the South African workplace and envisages the following changes to the EEA:

- The establishment of mandatory sector targets that all designated employers will have to comply with, or provide reasonable justification for non-compliance.
- A designated employer will only be awarded contracts or business from the State if it has been able to prove compliance with the EEA by having filed its Employment Equity report to the Department of Labour, has met the sectoral targets or provided reasonable justification for non-compliance, and does not have a judgment against it in either the Labour Court or the CCMA arising from having breached the provisions of the EEA.
- Designated employers that have met these requirements will be issued with a certificate from the Department of Labour proving compliance with the EEA, which certificate must be attached to all responses to requests for proposals from the State.
- Only employers who employ more than fifty employees will be defined as designated employers, regardless of the turnover that is generated by an employer.

24.2. Checklist of Do's and Don'ts

- Employers must properly assess the demographics of their workforce in order to identify the extent to which it is representative of the broader South African society.
- Employers must ensure that they compile employment equity plans and report on these to the Department of Labour as required.
- Reasonable accommodation for people from designated groups should be made in order to ensure that they enjoy equal opportunities and are equitably represented in the workplace.

25. RESOLUTION OF LABOUR, DISCRIMINATION AND EMPLOYMENT DISPUTES: LITIGATION, ARBITRATION, MEDIATION AND CONCILIATION

25.1. Internal Dispute Resolution Process

Minor, day-to-day employee complaints in the workplace in South Africa are generally resolved directly by supervisors or managers. For issues that cannot be resolved in this informal fashion, most medium and large South African employers have an internal grievance procedure pursuant to which employee complaints can be raised with escalating levels of management in the company. There are often two or three levels to which a grievance may be taken internally, with the purpose of the process being to explore the grievance and try and find a mutually acceptable resolution.

In unionized workplaces, workplace complaints are often raised through shop steward committees comprised of employees elected as representatives of the union in the workplace. There are often also formal dispute resolution processes provided for in collective agreements concluded between employers and their unions, which usually involve written notifications of complaints and a series of meetings to attempt to resolve them.

25.2. Mediation and Conciliation

The LRA's statutory dispute resolution mechanisms provided for dealing with employment disputes generally all entail a process of an employee referring a dispute (e.g., alleging unfair dismissal) to the CCMA or a bargaining council with jurisdiction, which body then sets a conciliation meeting presided over by one of its officials, at which an attempt must be made to resolve the dispute by agreement. If that attempt fails, the dispute can then be referred to arbitration or adjudication in the Labour Court, or the parties can resort to lawful industrial action (where the nature of the dispute is not susceptible to arbitration or adjudication). The statutory conciliation mechanisms have a fairly high success rate.

There is relatively little use made of private mediation and conciliation processes to resolve disputes, but it sometimes forms part of dispute resolution processes agreed between large employers and large unions or in substantial matters of national significance (such as national industrial action that may have a significant impact on the economy). Typically, everything said in the mediation process is privileged, and it cannot be used against either party in any formal proceedings. The mediator does not have any power to make any binding determination in respect of the dispute, but if the parties come to an agreement, the agreement is enforceable. The costs of the mediator are generally borne by the parties equally.

25.3. Arbitration

Compulsory statutory arbitration is the form of dispute resolution that is applied in the overwhelming majority of formal employment disputes. Under the LRA, disputes about the alleged unfairness of a dismissal for misconduct or incapacity have to be arbitrated (assuming the statutory conciliation process failed to resolve the dispute). Such arbitrations (which are conducted either by the CCMA or a bargaining council with jurisdiction over the employer) are required to be conducted fairly and quickly and must deal with the substantial merits of the dispute with the minimum of legal formalities.

Legal representation in arbitrations about dismissal for misconduct or incapacity is prohibited unless both parties and the arbitrator agree, or if there are unusual circumstances relating to the matter which would make it unreasonable to deny a party legal representation. Most arbitrations are therefore conducted by a manager representing the employer and the employee him or herself. The employee can be represented by a trade union official. Most arbitrations are concluded within a day unless the parties are legally represented, in which case the matter usually takes longer. Legal costs are very rarely awarded in arbitration, even where a party has been completely successful.

Arbitration awards made by the CCMA or bargaining council arbitrators are final and binding on the parties, and there is no appeal therefrom. Arbitration awards are susceptible to review, but this is only in instances where the arbitrator has committed some material, procedural irregularity, misconduct in relation to his or her duties or where it can be shown that no reasonable decision-maker in the position of the arbitrator could have come to the conclusion to which he or she did.

Private arbitration (i.e., outside of the compulsory CCMA or bargaining council arbitration) is used by some large employers with large unions as part of a collectively bargained dispute resolution mechanism tailored to the specific needs of those parties.

Some employers and employees make use of a mechanism provided for in the LRA known as an enquiry by arbitration to obtain a final and binding decision on serious disciplinary matters. By agreement between the employer and employee, an arbitrator is appointed to determine whether the employee is guilty of misconduct, and if so, whether he or she should be dismissed. The arbitrator's award is final and binding on both parties. The procedure obtains a quick and final resolution of the disciplinary issue, as it avoids the employer having to deal with a further post-termination arbitration at the CCMA or a bargaining council.

25.4. Litigation

There is no jury system in South Africa. Courts, including those dealing with employment disputes, are presided over by judges alone.

The Labour Court is a court of equivalent standing to South Africa's High Courts. Employment disputes that have to be heard by the Labour Court are automatically unfair dismissals, mass retrenchment dismissal disputes, strike dismissals, unfair discrimination disputes and alleged or threatened violations of constitutional rights arising from employment and labour relations.

Legal representation is a right in Labour Court proceedings, and dispute resolution through litigation is the most expensive form of dispute resolution.

Due to substantial backlogs that have developed at the Labour Courts, it can take a year for a dispute that requires oral evidence to be adjudicated by the Labour Court. Of late, the administrative processes at the Labour Court have improved, and this backlog is being cleared, with the result that the delay in obtaining a date for the trial is becoming shorter. The proceedings are formal, adversarial trial proceedings with formal evidence under oath and cross-examination.

Labour Court decisions can be appealed to the LAC (subject to obtaining leave to appeal). If the matter and issue involve a constitutional question, further appeal lies to the Constitutional Court (subject again to leave to appeal being granted).

Before a trial date will be set in Labour Court proceedings, the parties are required to conduct a pre-trial conference between themselves (or presided over by a judge if this becomes necessary), at which the parties are expected to endeavour to reach agreement on issues and matters of evidence that will streamline the time spent in trial. The parties are also required to consider whether the matter can be settled when conducting the pre-trial conference.

25.5. Fines, Penalties and Damages

In dismissal disputes, arbitrators have the power to award reinstatement to an employee, which may be retroactive.

The compensation awards and orders that can be made by arbitrators or judges vary depending on the nature of the dispute. As indicated above, ordinary unfair dismissal disputes have a maximum financial compensation limit of twelve months pay, although if the employee has been retrospectively reinstated and he or she has been out of employment for longer than twelve months, the full amount of the back pay is still owed.

In automatically unfair dismissal cases that come before the Labour Court, the court may award reinstatement (which can be retroactive) or financial compensation subject to a maximum amount equivalent to twenty-four months of the remuneration earned by the employer when he or she was dismissed. A successful party in Labour Court proceedings is not always awarded his or her legal costs, especially if there is an ongoing relationship between the parties (e.g., where the applicant is the union party recognized at the workplace, and the respondent is the employer).

Awards of compensation are separate from any other damages that an employee may be able to prove in relation to the unfairness on the part of the employer. Damages (e.g., for loss of income or defamation or medical costs) that can be proved by an employee are not subject to the twelve or twenty-four months' pay limits referred above.

For unfair labour practice disputes, arbitrators have the power to determine such disputes on the terms that the arbitrator deems reasonable. This may include ordering reinstatement or re-employment or compensation where compensation could be up to twelve months' remuneration.

25.6. Checklist of Do's and Don'ts

Employers should:

- establish a simple internal grievance procedure to deal with internal disputes. The procedure need not be formal;
- consider providing for an option to invoke pre-dismissal arbitration in the employment contracts of appropriate categories of employees;

- familiarize themselves with CCMA conciliation and arbitration proceedings as they may have to appear there without legal representation;
- not assume that they can simply get rid of a problematic employee by firing him or her and then settling afterwards by paying compensation, as the primary remedy available to employees fired without a fair reason is reinstatement into employment.

26. EMPLOYER RECORD-KEEPING, DATA PROTECTION, AND EMPLOYEE ACCESS TO PERSONNEL FILES AND RECORDS

26.1. Overview

There is currently relatively limited regulation of how long employers are required to retain personnel records. In practice, many employers keep such records for longer periods than the minimum required.

Comprehensive legislation (the POPI Act) regulating data protection was enacted at the end of 2013, but it is still to become effective on a date to be announced in due course. POPI is designed to regulate the POPI in the public and private sectors. It provides employees with a number of rights and employers with a number of obligations in relation to how information about the employees is handled. It is to be enforced by an Information Protection Regulator.

Under POPI, personal information may only be collected by an employer directly from and with the consent of the employee, who must be informed of the purpose of any collection, and who the intended recipients are when the information is collected. Personal information should also not be kept for longer than necessary to achieve the (permitted) purpose for which collected, and it must be distributed in a way which is compatible with the purpose for which it was collected. The employer must also take reasonable steps to ensure that the information is accurate, up-to-date and complete.

Under POPI, the employer must also take steps to protect its employees against risks of loss, damage or destruction of, or unauthorized access to, their personal information kept by the employer.

POPI does not require employers to register with a data protection agency or other government bodies, but an employer can only collect and store personal information about its employees if it has notified the Information Protection Regulator and the employees, and it is necessary or related to a lawful and permitted purpose under the legislation. It must also not unreasonably intrude on the privacy of the employee.

POPI considers the following information as special personal information for which there are additional protections: information concerning children, religious or philosophical beliefs, race or ethnic origin, trade union membership, political opinions, health, sexual life or criminal behaviour. This special personal information may not be processed by an employer unless specifically permitted under exemptions provided for in the legislation. Examples of exemptions are processing race information where this is required for the employer to comply with laws designed to protect or advance persons disadvantaged by unfair discrimination, which would include the EEA which contains affirmative action obligations for designated employers.

POPI prohibits cross-border (and onward) transfers of personal information to countries that do not have substantially similar protections for the information (except under limited circumstances). Such transfers must be notified to the Information Protection Regulator and the employee, and the employee's consent to the transfer is generally required. The transfer must be necessary for contractual arrangements involving the employee.

Employers should plan for compliance with POPI.

Under the Electronic Communications and Transactions Act (ECTA), an employer may also choose to comply voluntarily with certain principles regarding the collection, storage and dissemination of personal information in electronic format. These principles are codified in sections 50 and 51 of ECTA.

26.2. Personnel Files

The BCEA requires written particulars of the essential terms of employment of an employee, together with records of the time worked and remuneration paid to the employee to be retained for three years.

Employers should also retain records in relation to their hiring, training and promotion practices (including details of the race, gender and disability status of the job applicants/employees involved) for the duration of their employment equity plans (which can range from one year to five years), so that they have these records available to substantiate their efforts made towards employment equity compliance in any review by the Department of Labour.

26.3. Confidentiality Rules

Under South Africa's constitutional and common law privacy laws, personal information in relation to which an employee has an expectation of privacy and which is kept by the employer in a personnel file must be kept confidential. An example of this would be medical information relating to the employee.

Under POPI, there are more specific statutory obligations on employers to keep personal information about employees safe and to prevent unauthorized access thereto.

26.4. Employee Access

In practice, most employees in South Africa do not request access to their personnel files and employers are reluctant to give employees such access.

Under POPI, however, employees will have a right to access their personal information held by the employer (including information in personnel files) and can demand to correct the information if it is found to be inaccurate.

27. REQUIRED NOTICES AND POSTINGS

27.1. Overview

Both the BCEA and the EEA place a duty on employers to inform employees of their rights under the Acts.

The BCEA requires that a statement, in the prescribed form, of the employee's rights must be displayed in the workplace where it can be read by employees, in the official languages which are spoken at the workplace (South Africa has eleven official languages, but in most workplaces only one or two of the languages are used).

The EEA requires an employer to display a notice, in the prescribed form, at the workplace where it can be read by employees, informing them about the provisions of the Act. The Regulations to the EEA contain a standard notice which summarizes the provisions of the Act and is to be displayed in all official languages. The notice (which includes the summary) can be obtained from the Government Printers as well as the local publishers of legislation.

In addition, the EEA requires an employer who has an employment equity plan to make a copy thereof available to its employees for copying and consultation. Designated employers[13] are also required to display in each of their workplaces:

13. Designated employers are defined as employers that employ more than fifty people or whose annual turnover is equal to or more than the scheduled amount, which depends on the sector in which the employer operates.

– the most recent employment equity report;
– any compliance order, arbitration award or order of the Labour Court concerning the provisions of the Act relating to that employer; and
– any other document concerning the Act as may be prescribed.

Regulations issued under the EEA also require employers to notify the Department of Labour of any changes to their trade names, status as a designed employer, contact details or any other major changes, including mergers, acquisitions and insolvencies.

Collective agreements regulating a union's rights in the workplace (usually referred to as a recognition agreement) usually give a union the right to display their notices at designated places in the workplace.

27.2. Checklist of Do's and Don'ts

– The BCEA and EEA may be amended from time to time, and it is important to ensure that an updated summary of these Acts is displayed in the workplace at all times.
– When providing trade unions with a right to display their notices in the workplace, make this right subject to the written approval of the notices prior to being displayed.
– Allocate a specific place(s) in the workplace where the notices may be displayed by recognized trade unions, and reserve the right to refuse the display of any notices at the employer's sole discretion.

www.ingramcontent.com/pod-product-compliance
Lightning Source LLC
Chambersburg PA
CBHW071351230926
51846CB00002B/506
9789403525044